The Women's Guide to Legal Rights

The Women's Guide to Legal Rights

Jane Shay Lynch
Sara Lyn Smith

Contemporary Books, Inc.
Chicago

Library of Congress Cataloging in Publication Data

Lynch, Jane Shay.
  The women's guide to legal rights.

  Includes index.
  1. Women—Legal status, laws, etc.—United States—
Popular works. 2. Women's rights—United States.
I. Smith, Sara Lyn, joint author. II. Title.
KF478.Z9L96   346'.73'013   78-73669
ISBN 0-8092-7368-3
ISBN 0-8092-7367-5 pbk.

Published by Contemporary Books, Inc.
180 North Michigan Avenue, Chicago, Illinois 60601
Manufactured in the United States of America
Library of Congress Catalog Card Number: 78-73669
International Standard Book Number: ISBN 0-8092-7368-3
                              ISBN 0-8092-7367-5 pbk.
Published simultaneously in Canada by
Beaverbooks
953 Dillingham Road
Pickering, Ontario L1W 1Z7
Canada

FOR: Ursula A. Day and Patty Klein

Contents

ACKNOWLEDGMENTS

Special thanks to Bernadette Doran for her editorial consultation

Thanks to the following lawyers, students, and organizations for their assistance:

Julie Badel
John Corwin
Lisa Gertz
Martha Goddard
Patricia Handlin
Esther O. Kegan
Mary Kelly
Michelle Lowrance
Darlene Raudabaugh
Becca Schumaker
Louis Sohn
Karen Wellisch, Editor/Publisher
   The Spokeswoman
Sandra Frank, Director, Women's Bureau,
   U.S. Dept. of Labor, and Joanne Olson,
   U.S. Department of Labor

Preface

A Word from the Authors

The area of women's rights under the law is now so detailed that an encyclopedia could barely contain it all. This book seeks to point out some of the most important issues affecting women. It is meant to be a guide to the legal areas where women do have significant rights, and to those where more legislative action is needed.

By having a general feel for your various rights, you may be better able to seek the many remedies available to you. And you also may be better aware of issues you'd like to have your elected representatives resolve.

We hope to help clear up some of the myths, help clarify some of your general options, but we can't possibly provide you with legal *advice* through these pages. Every woman's factual situation is unique, and the laws in every area of women's rights are changing rapidly. Your lawyer can determine with you what you should do in any given legal situation—based on the facts of *your* case, the laws of *your* state, and the way the courts of your state are interpreting and applying these laws. No book can do this for you.

We hope to help you educate yourself about the present status of your rights, but we must caution you that this is by no means a "how-to" book. You may hear about some of your rights here, but it's your lawyer's job to see how and when they apply to *you*.

How the Law Works

What is the structure of the law? Throughout this book, we'll be referring to "the law," meaning state and federal legislation; U.S. Supreme Court decisions; federal and state court decisions, including appellate court decisions; common law; executive orders; and, less technically, regulations of administrative agencies. "The law" is made by all these bodies.

If *federal* legislation is passed, your lawsuit demanding your rights under federal laws is brought in federal court. Or, even if there is *not* federal legislation, you're entitled to go to federal court in a variety of situations, including to argue that your Constitutional rights have been violated. In both cases, the losing party can appeal the decision to a federal appeals court and to the U.S. Supreme Court.

The analogous situation holds true regarding your rights under state legislation and your state constitution. State court is also the place you bring "common law" actions. That is, no statute exists—no legislation has been drafted and passed to deal with the point—but the courts have ruled in this area, and their decisions alone are viewed as "the law" here. State court decisions are appealed to state appeals court, then to the state supreme courts. From there, further review can be requested from the U.S. Supreme Court.

As a practical matter, the U.S. Supreme Court hears only a tiny fraction of all the cases sent there in hopes the high court will rule on them. For every 5,000 cases where review is sought, the Supreme Court hears only two or three! How do they decide on which cases to hear? Generally, where there's great legal uncertainty about a particular issue—evidenced by seemingly inconsistent rulings in local courts—the U.S. Supreme Court agrees to hear the case and to rule. It is generally *not* the practice of the Supreme Court to take a case just because the particular individual has been treated unfairly by a lower court. Because there are only nine U.S. Supreme Court Justices, they generally must use their limited resources to decide the cases with maximum impact—so that the state and federal courts as well as Congress can be uniformly guided.

As to the Executive Orders, these are "presidential proclamations." There are two such orders that affect women, particularly women in the employment sphere. Administrative agencies—including the Equal Employment Opportunity Commission (EEOC), the U.S. Department of Labor, the Federal Trade Commission, even the U.S. Patent and Trademark Office—all have "regulations." While a regulation isn't technically a law, it's usually given credence by the courts.

The law can change or "develop" *every day*. State and federal legislative bodies draft new laws—or bills or acts, as they're often interchangeably called; courts interpret legislation; agency regulations and courts interpret *other* courts! Sometimes the appeals judge says the lower court was wrong—but this "appellate" opinion might not be resolved for as long as a year. And, meanwhile, the lower court's decision is viewed as law! Sometimes the court itself decides that its previous interpretations are wrong—that, in view of the way society has changed, someone should not be penalized *today* for conduct that was considered "immoral" twenty years ago.

For these reasons, this book can steer you to certain issues—but the *answers* to the hypothetical questions raised may change! How to keep up? If you have a *particular* problem, seek legal counsel. If you're just interested in this area of the law, there are extremely competent women's groups organized around almost every issue affecting women and their legal rights. They'll be glad to provide you with up-to-the-minute information. Some of these groups are noted throughout this book—and you can learn of *other* groups through them, too.

What is the lawyer's job in all of this? The lawyer keeps up with the changes and determines whether the facts of *your* situation are covered by existing law. *A small change in your factual situation can often be a* big *factor in the outcome!* The lawyer urges the judge to apply certain interpretations of the law to decide in your favor. Your opponent's lawyer tries to convince the judge that the facts of your circumstances aren't covered by existing law or that the law can't be interpreted in your favor. The larger part of a lawyer's day is spent in "preventive" counseling—advising you how to accomplish a specific result without risking liability, preparing contracts and other documents, reviewing documents before advising you to sign.

In our age of specialization, no lawyer—and not even every "general practitioner"—is familiar with the law in *every* area. If your lawyer is *not* up on the fast-developing areas of law affecting women's rights, she can research the problem. *All* lawyers do this; very few problems can be resolved on an "off-the-top-of-one's-head" basis. Or, she can refer you to a lawyer with expertise in the specific field.

How this Book Works

In the law—as in real life—issues can't always be "compartmentalized," and many issues are woven in with many others. Marriage and credit, child custody and divorce, marriage and wills, pregnancy and insurance—and, of course, taxes and just about everything else—blur neat lines of demarcation. Basically, we've tried to separate the issues into four distinct categories:

1. *Home, Family and Personal Choice*—Where cohabitation, surname rights, marriage, divorce, child custody, abortion, even wills pose various legal issues.

2. *Employment*—Most women—single or married, mothers or not—work. And most women are still paid less than most men, plus have a more difficult crack at advancement. Consequently, employment rights is an area where the law is changing and expanding rapidly. Besides employment rights, there are new *unemployment* rights, Social Security rights, pension rights, even tax rights!

3. *The Marketplace*—The days are long—but not *that* long—gone since women have lawfully been refused service in public bars and restaurants. But it's been fairly recent since a woman's money

has looked as attractive as a man's, and it took federal legislation, the new Equal Credit Opportunity Act, to make that so. Similar problems are apparent in the insurance industry where again, our dollar doesn't seem to buy as much as a man's and here too, the law is beginning to change. Consequently, credit rights and insurance issues provide the major focus of this section.

4. *Crimes Against Women*—While rape and spouse-abuse aren't exclusively women's burden, women *statistically* are more often victimized in these ways. What are our rights—and what can we expect from the law in these unfortunately not-so-uncommon situations? These issues are explored in the final section.

**The Women's
Guide to
Legal Rights**

1

Home and Family

Cohabitation

Joe and I have been involved for two years. Since we're not into marriage, we've decided that we want to live together. It's legal, isn't it?

In most states, no!

That's hard to believe when you consider that over 1.5 million people, according to the U.S. Bureau of the Census, and more every day are moving under the same roof without bothering to marry first. But nevertheless it's against the law in the majority of states.

And *every* state in the union has some form of "morality legislation" that, while not specifically banning cohabitation, makes illegal much of what you'd do together anyway. Topping the list is "fornication," which a state usually defines as having sexual intercourse with someone you're not married to. Some states say once is enough; others specify that the parties live together and do it habitually for it to constitute a crime.

A shade slightly different is "adultery." In some states' cross-eyed view, it's *not* criminal if the man is married, but *only* if the female *is*. And adultery can still be dredged up in some states as grounds for divorce.

While legislation against fornication and adultery is usually directed at heterosexual couples, there are other varieties more specifically targeted at homosexual partners. Sodomy, fellatio, cunnilingus—in general, oral and anal intercourse—are crimes in several states, unless you happen to have benefit, as they say, of clergy.

Bigamy and polygamy are crimes in some places—so be sure your divorce is final! And the unlawfulness of "lewd and lascivious" behavior, operating a "house of prostitution," a "disorderly house," or a "bawdy house" round out the law's efforts to legislate morality in an attempt to protect the "sacred" married state against those who would "abuse" it.

Since that archaic position includes people living together, there are indeed states where cohabitation is a crime. It's usually defined as two people who live together without being married but who openly act as though they were. Some states don't even require you to live in the same house together—the appearances of wedded bliss are enough.

Are these prohibitions a *real* threat to cohabiting couples? Well, it would be irresponsible to say absolutely not. The laws are on the books, and they *can* be enforced although, with lifestyles changing so rapidly, if the police and the prosecutors rushed around enforcing "morality legislation," they'd have precious little time to do much else. As lifestyles change, cultural attitudes do too, and people are feeling much differently these days about sex, marriage, and morality from the way they did when all those prohibitory laws were passed. Should those laws be enforced, the purpose is usually to harass gays or for some ulterior motive, not generally to disrupt an innocuous love-nest.

How can cohabitation be a crime? I thought cohabiting could be considered common-law marriage.

Only a handful of states still recognize common-law marriage which is said to exist after you've lived together and represented yourselves to the world as husband and wife. In common-law states because the two of you consider yourselves married, the states do too and only divorce will legally dissolve your relationship. Of the states that do acknowledge common-law marriages, many require a certain number of years the two of you must live together before the common knot is legally tied.

Then, what's this about the Lee Marvin case?

As this book goes to press, the court has not yet decided whether Lee Marvin will have to make a property settlement with his ex-live-in roommate, Michelle Triola Marvin. (She'd even adopted his surname.) The case is a landmark nonetheless because the California Supreme Court did say that "unmarried spouses" could acquire the same property rights as marrieds. The court's decision was based mainly on an "oral contract" theory—it was conceivable that Michelle did agree with Lee that, if she gave up her career, he would support her. Said the court, in effect, if the party suing can prove such a contract was made, then property rights can be awarded.

Triola may be entitled to support, not because she was a common-law wife, but because she was an ex-roommate with rights.

The precedent is here, but, since alimony is only awarded in 14 percent of all divorces, it's unlikely that a whopping percentage of roomies will fare much better.

When will the courts probably step in? When cohabiting couples have merged their funds to buy a car, a boat, a state-of-the-art stereo system, or other property, or when one partner has forsaken a good job to tend the kids.

Can I get child support from my mate if we lived together out of wedlock?

Maybe!

If a "paternity action" is brought within the "statute of limitations"—the time period required to bring suit—the answer is generally yes. But what if you're beyond that time allowance and missed your chance, or you simply want your child's father to accept the same financial responsibility he'd have to accept for his child if you were divorcing?

Under a recent Illinois decision, Victoria Hewitt, 37, established that, when she became pregnant, her mate told her that he thought of her as his wife and always would. He also told Hewitt that he would share his life, his future earnings, and his property with her. The couple then announced to their respective parents that they were married.

The Illinois case cited the Lee Marvin decision to point out that in Hewitt's case an oral contract for support had effectively been entered into. The court concluded that child support payments had been contemplated under that oral contract as well. The 1970 census found eight times as many non-marital relationships as ten years earlier; therefore, the Illinois Court stated, "The courts should be prepared to deal realistically and fairly with problems that exist in the life of our day."

I've never been married and don't ever intend to be. But I do want to live with my partner. What are some ways the property issues might be resolved?

Resolve them now—before the first shirt ever goes into the space you made in your sweater drawer!

As you saw in the Marvin case, the California courts acknowledged that, had Lee and Michelle made an oral contract, it could be enforced. But even better is a *written* contract—made before you combine households and while you're still on the friendliest, most loving terms—expressly stating what belongs, or will belong, to whom whether you stay together or stray apart. If the contract is based on "the exchange of sexual favors," it won't hold up in court, because prostitution is illegal. But a contract you'd draw up for the purposes of divvying things up would likely pass muster in the courts, if properly made.

How can you divvy? You have a lot of options. Real estate can be held by both of you. A mortgage in both names makes you both responsible. He won't feel as though he's a renter in your house and you won't get stuck with payments if the relationship cracks at the foundation. And, even if the two of you aren't married, ECOA protects you from discrimination in obtaining a mortgage in both names. Besides, the creditors are on your side already; they always prefer two parties to one for debt-paying responsibility.

The two of you can hold *property* two different ways: as joint tenants, or as tenants in common. With joint tenancy, *both* of you own the *whole* farm or savings account together. If one dies, the other automatically gets the whole package. With tenancy in common, you each own *half* interest, but you both have the right to "possess" the entire property. If you die, your interest passes to your heirs, *not* to your roommate. (And see p. 32 on wills)

If you live in a community property state, the property laws and regulations probably won't affect you—unless you eventually decide to take that long walk down the aisle—because they apply to marrieds only.

If we have kids while we live together, what are some of the problems we might encounter?

In the first place, the children will be considered "illegitimate" in the eyes of the law. And, as a result, you'll have no automatic right to child support from the father, unless you go through a paternity suit and prove he's the dad. Giving your "love child" his surname won't help, that doesn't *prove* paternity.

What about inheritance? If dad makes a will, you can be sure your child will inherit from her father, but, without a will, the state laws go churning into effect. Generally then, the child will not inherit from the father's side unless the father has "legitimized" or adopted her. And different states have different requirements for that; some say a father's acknowledgment in writing in the presence of witnesses or a justice of the peace is good enough. The U.S. Supreme Court recently okayed a New York law providing that an illegitimate child may *not* inherit from the natural father unless paternity has been established in court during the father's lifetime! More states can be expected to draft harsh inheritance laws accordingly. So check with your lawyer for your state's particular procedure.

If you die, will the father be able to get automatic custody of the child? No! According to the Supreme Court, a "biological" father is entitled only to a *hearing* to see if he's a good father! Here's what happened in the case that led to that decision. A man and woman had lived together almost twenty years and, during that time, had four children together. When the woman died, the state stepped in and told the father, in effect, that he had no more rights to the kids than a stranger would! But the case climbed up to the Supreme Court, who said the state was wrong, sort of. The father had first dibbies, but only if he could *prove* he was a fit father. In a legal marriage, by comparison, the natural father wouldn't have to prove his fitness to get custody of his own children.

What are some of the benefits of marriage that I forego as a cohabitor?

Since marriage, and only marriage, assumes that the wife and children need protection, you're giving up most of those "protective" rights. You lose your "homestead rights," for example, those state laws that protect a certain portion of a married couple's assets from the ravages of creditors should the husband die.

Unless you have a will or unless you and your partner own property in joint tenancy, those worldly goods will pass to specific relatives; they will not automatically go to your partner. Depending on the laws of your state, he may be bypassed for your brothers or sisters—even for the state itself. Your best bet is to make a will in order to have your wishes respected.

You can't get "automatic" extended insurance coverage the way married folks do. Many insurance companies have policies that cover spouses and children, but not cohabitors. Getting insurance in the first place can be difficult and most insurance companies won't cover your partner's personal property loss. It's tempting to know that it's usually cheaper to buy insurance jointly, but don't succumb unless the insurance company knows what your situation is; otherwise, they may void the policy when they find out. The best bet is for both of you to get your own insurance.

Your spouse can't be forced to testify against you at a criminal trial, but your roommate certainly can be. If one of you is in military service, there's an entire regiment of benefits—pensions, services and a lot more— that would be yours if you were married, but they can't be yours because you're not. And if you're not yet a citizen, you could be deported for immoral conduct.

Now for the good news: There are at least two definite advantages of living together out of wedlock and the big one is taxes. Yes, it's true that you can't claim your roommate as a dependent for a deduction. But your combined tax burden is very likely to be much lower than marrieds'. In a household where both partners are working, chances are that, if they're not married, they'll get to keep the same healthy chunk that the ball-and-chain group will have to fork over to Uncle Sam. But, before cancelling that clergyman, check with an accountant or tax lawyer! The IRS is peculiar, and at some income brackets, it's the "single couple" who pays through the snout.

And, if you've noticed a few more senior citizens spurning the altar, the reason could be Social Security. Right now, there are the same kind of funny quirks in the Social Security regulations that there are in the IRS formulas. So, many older folks are cohabiting because the Social Security benefits they live on would *decrease* if they said "I do"!

Marriage

My married friends all squabble about the division of household labor. I'm planning to marry, and I wonder whether a marriage contract might prevent such upsets.

If your husband doesn't pick up his socks, it's unlikely you'll head off an argument by referring to paragraph six, clause eight of your marriage agreement.

But a marriage contract *can* help, because it sets out clearly each spouse's expectations. It can avoid what marriage counselors refer to as the "hidden agenda"; he secretly assumes, perhaps subcon-

sciously, that he'll be able to talk you out of your job after the babies
arrive or you secretly assume you'll be able to pry him away from
those regular Sunday dinners with his folks.

Are these "non-monetary" contractual obligations enforceable?
Right now, it's doubtful. But the laws are changing and it may be
that by the time you're ready to tell it to the judge, the judge will
be ready to listen.

And, to be enforceable, they'll have to pass "contracts law" muster. Since the law generally requires a bargained-for exchange, a list
of "I agree to wash the dishes, the dog, and the car" will probably
not suffice. In other words, you'll have to come up with trade-
offs—"I'll wash the dog once a week because you'll take it for a walk
once a night."

Should you do your contract yourself? If you seriously intend the
agreement to be legal and binding, take it to a lawyer for finalizing
after you and your fiancé decide on the points to be included. Some
lawyers have speculated that enforceability can be enhanced by providing for liquidated damages—cash amounts to be paid if promises
are broken. Why? The judge probably won't issue an order requiring Max to diaper the baby on Monday, but he/she may order Max
to pay Myrna the reasonable cash value of the neglected task. You
might discuss this strategy with your own attorney.

*I'm thirty-five years old and have begun to build my empire. My fiancé is
twenty-two, cute and understanding, but his ability to support himself
is, well, undocumented to date. We're both realists about the divorce statistics, and I wonder whether a contract now might spare me financial
anxiety later.*

It certainly might!

Unlike the more recent contracts for division of housework and
childcare services, pre-marriage contracts that set forth the way the
goodies will be divided should you divorce have *long* been enforced
by the courts.

Antenuptial—"before-the-wedding"—agreements are often entered into by older couples with children from previous relation-

ships. They want to be sure their estates—money and property, however modest or immodest—aren't distributed in the form of alimony instead of being available for inheritance by their children.

Agreements have also been used by the super-rich to keep from lining the pockets of the spouse whose ball-and-chain term is less than a lifetime. And, where one person has substantial wealth and the other doesn't, the cold contract can serve as a convenient buffer to those chilly chats that start with, "I think you married me for my money."

Why *pre*-marriage contracts? Because traditionally it's been the woman who's signed away her rights to substantial alimony. And the courts have historically recognized that women—once upon a time, at least—were dependent on their husband's generosity for a living. So they might well be expected to sign just about anything put before them by their loving mates. Nevertheless, if the court was satisfied that the financially or emotionally "weaker" spouse's interests were represented by her own counsel, a contract between husband and wife for division of property could be upheld.

If you decide to enter a "division of property" agreement only after you've walked down the aisle, make sure a lawyer shows up on the groom's side as well as the bride's. For the ultimate enforceability of the document, it's important for both spouses, and particularly the "weaker" one, to be represented by counsel—to help avoid a charge of coercion in enforcement of the contract.

I'm not employed. My husband earns plenty, but he hides it. Sick? Maybe. But otherwise we get along fine and I don't really want a divorce. Am I entitled to support?

Yes and no.

In law, there's the saying, "For every right, there must be a remedy." In other words: What good are laws on the books if you can't enforce them in court when they're violated? A married woman's right to support usually flounders in this no-person's-land of remedy-less right!

Yes, the laws of virtually every state require a working spouse to support his or her mate. But, no, the courts of most states do *not* intervene to require the skinflint to spend his scratch for even the basics—such as indoor plumbing, as a wife learned in a famous case on this point. Your lawyer can best advise you about your state's practices.

One exception is that, if he can't be required to support you while you stay, he may be required to support you if you leave! Once the wife has petitioned for "separate maintenance"—a legal separation, often a prelude to divorce— the courts will compel her husband to provide support checks, if she needs them and other qualifications are met.

And, of course, if you *charge* necessities to him, he'll probably have to fork over the bucks.

The first lesson: Sometimes a fool and his money are *not* so easily parted, unless his spouse files for divorce. The second lesson: Anti-ERA forces argue that ERA will cut off the wife's right to be supported in her marriage. Not only is this a lie—the laws of many states are already "unisex," requiring the needy spouse to be provided for by the income-producing mate—but, generally, a still-married person's "right to support" isn't worth the lawbooks it's printed in.

Right to Own Surname

I want to keep my surname when I marry. May the law automatically thrust my husband's name upon me when I say "I do"?

In every state, you're entitled to be known by any name you choose—as long as you do it consistently, and don't do it for fraudulent purposes. In a dwindling number of states, you *do* have to fill out a form to prevent his name from becoming your own! How to find out? When you go to get your marriage license, these few states require you to indicate at that time that you don't want to take your husband's surname.

I've been at my job for several years, and I recently got married. Although I'm keeping my own surname, my employer has changed my name on the payroll and other personnel records to my husband's surname. He says the law requires him to do this. Can he be right?

No!

In 1977, a federal appeals court decided that an employer's "name-change" policy—requiring married female employees to use their husband's surnames on all personnel forms or be suspended from employment—was indeed sex discrimination, in violation of Title VII of the Civil Rights Act.

I've never taken my husband's surname, but I took my driving test and passed. Imagine my surprise when I got my license issued in my husband's surname! Administrative snafu? I thought so, until the licensing bureau told me that that was their procedure, and that the license couldn't be issued in my own name! Can they do this?

It depends on where you live!

Over the last few years, the issue has been litigated in Alabama and Kentucky, two states that apparently don't go along with the "rose-by-any-other-name" theory. Both states have the regulation that a driver's license must be issued to a married woman *only* in her husband's surname. In 1972, the U. S. Supreme Court ok'd the Alabama regulation without specifically naming their reasons. Later a similar challenge was brought up—and a similar decision was brought down—in Kentucky courts.

Some states, on the other hand, require that you notify particular state agencies—either when you've married and adopted your husband's surname, or when you've shed his surname and have re-claimed your own. You're required, in these states, to re-register your motor vehicle, change your driver's license, and voter's registration. But, while the laws generally provide for penalties for failure to comply, they're seldom enforced.

What if I want to change back to my maiden name, or to select a new surname other than my husband's? Must I go to court?

Not in most states! An exception at present is the state of Maine.

Generally, it's sufficient to change your name by common law, not statutory methods. Meaning? Where the common-law change is applicable, it's enough to change your name by simply changing it! Just put it on your bank accounts, driver's license, voter's registration, passport, charge accounts, whatever. And, by the way, your husband's consent is *not* required.

In states where common-law method is allowed, why do women bother with a court procedure? Sometimes having a piece of paper—a court order—makes your name change seem more legitimate to bureaucrats, employers, even family. Women who've experienced hassles having their common-law name change taken seriously have gone the court route because it was easier than arguing about it over and over again.

Incidentally, the same principles apply when your spouse wants to take *your* surname, when you hyphenate both your names (Jennifer and Michael Carrington-Smothers), or come up with a new surname (Jennifer and Michael Carrothers).

Some women prefer to use their husband's surname during marriage, but want to resume their premarital moniker when they divorce. It's become such a common practice that the divorce laws of many states now give you the right to have a formal name change right along with your formal split-up.

If I decide to go through name-change court proceedings, what's involved?

In some states, you can ask the court for a change of name *pro se*, on your own, and without a lawyer. You can simply go to the clerk's office in your local courthouse and request the necessary forms. Personnel there should be able to explain what the costs are and what the exact procedure will be.

If you have a problem, or if you live in a state where *pro se* isn't allowed, try to contact your local feminist organization, the ACLU, or a "people's" law group. They should be able to refer you to a lawyer who's familiar with this area of the law.

If I remarry, can my children take my new spouse's surname without being adopted by him?

Usually. This can be done, again, either by common-law adoption of his name or by a court proceeding.

However, in a *court* proceeding, the natural father may have the opportunity to object. If he does, the courts will probably look into the best interests of the child, sometimes asking the child, in chambers, his or her preference. If the child's natural father has made himself scarce through much of the child's life, the courts are usually more agreeable to the change.

The courts may also look favorably on the change if the bid for a formal name change is made after your children have established a family relationship with their new stepfather, or you have a child with your new husband and your older child expresses an interest in a name change to make him feel more a part of the new family.

My husband is very bitter about my filing for our divorce. When we married, I took his surname and have always used it. All my professional contacts know me by this name, and I want to keep it. He says he'll take legal action to force me to stop using his surname. Do I have the right to my name in this situation?

In a recent case, a woman professional was faced with legal action by her ex-husband, who sought to "take his name back" from her after a long-standing marriage. The fact that, to this woman, his name was *her* name, the name she'd used for years, persuaded the court. To require her to relinquish it, the court reasoned, would be unreasonable. Case closed for this woman.

But the court did *not* give an opinion about whether there might be circumstances in which a name *could* reasonably be wrested from a woman at her ex-husband's request. However, lawyers working in this specialty doubt that there are any circumstances where a woman's right to her married name could be constitutionally terminated.

Divorce

My husband and I don't get along and haven't for years. He's not a bad guy; we just don't feel a commitment to each other anymore. But is this enough, legally, for a judge to untie our knot?

In most states, yes!

Imagine if all, or even half, the divorced people you know got that way because the law had required *proof* of their incorrigible nastiness. Could you ever feel safe at a cocktail party again?

Right now, forty-five states have adopted *some* form of no-fault divorce. The exceptions: Illinois, Massachusetts, Mississippi, Pennsylvania, and South Dakota. Even in these "exceptional" states, things have been liberalized so that, for example, in Illinois, you don't lose your right to divorce when *both* parties are at fault. Previously, the party suing for divorce had to be "good," the party sued "bad." Now *both* can be rotten to the core!

Many states, including Arizona, California, Colorado, Delaware, Florida, Iowa, Kentucky, Michigan, Minnesota, Missouri, Nebraska, Oregon, and Washington, have gone *exclusively* "no-fault." The traditional grounds for divorce—adultery, physical or mental cruelty, desertion, alcoholism, drug addiction, felony conviction, and impotence—are completely *irrelevant* in these states. So those who want out, get out!

Other states require incompatibility coupled up with one of the more exotic grounds—mental cruelty, for example. And some states have procedural impediments to the dance-away divorce. New York, for example, permits no-fault divorce, but the laws require the couple to live apart for a year, after a court-approved separation agreement, before the divorce can be finalized.

What if you happen to be in a state where grounds are all or nothing? Here's an example: In Illinois, a hold-out against "no-fault," a whopping percentage of divorces are brought on grounds of "mental cruelty." But no extensive or unusual forms of psychic torture need be trotted out for the judge. In fact, where both spouses have resigned themselves to the divorce, courtroom proceedings can take less time than you need to hard-boil an egg.

Yes, there's a law on the Illinois books stating that, if both spouses collude and *manufacture* grounds, no divorce can be granted. As a practical matter, however, the judges aren't aggressive in sniffing out conspiracies.

The most persuasive argument in favor of no-fault has been that it eliminates the regrettable travesty during which time the spouses and their lawyers fudge the truth about grounds, while the judges courteously refrain from extensive probing.

What about alimony and child support? Who gets the stereo? And what happens to our tax rebate—and our debts?

Contrary to popular belief most divorced women are *not* awarded alimony. And of the 14 percent who *do* get an alimony or maintenance award, the amounts are low—averaging less than $3,000 a year.

Who gets alimony? Typically, the woman with children who has been married a long time. Younger women are sometimes awarded alimony, especially if the wife abandoned school or career for a more mundane job so she could put hubby through grad school. In these cases, the courts may limit the amount and duration of the alimony to allow the woman to readjust to, and retrain for, the wage-earning world. And most states *don't* require the alimony-seeking party to be blameless.

But child support is a different matter. All states try to see that the children are adequately financially cared for, and they don't hesitate to award child support payments, even when alimony is *not* awarded. The payments aren't generally in keeping with the actual cost of raising children, and sometimes only amount to 20 percent or less of the father's take-home pay. More than 50 percent is practically unheard of.

What about property? In community property states, almost all money and property acquired after the wedding are viewed as belonging equally to husband and wife. Yes, even if one spouse stays home while the other works for an income, that income is the property of *both* spouses. And so is the car, no matter whose name is on the title, and the house, and on and on. Does this mean that, in a community property state, you'll get half his income—or he'll get half of *yours*—*after* the divorce? No. But you *may* get half the goodies lying around the house and the bank account—and half the house—all originating with that equally shared income.

What about the majority of states which have no community property laws. Even in a *non*-community property state, money and "things" are generally viewed as "marital property" if acquired after that walk down the aisle. It doesn't matter that *he* signed the check for the dinette set, that *his* name is on the title of the car, or that *he* bought the sofa on *his* VISA account. It's "marital property," and it's generally viewed as both of *yours* until adjudicated otherwise.

If it sounds like a mirror image of the community property laws, it's not. Despite a seeming similarity, there's a "downside." Why? It's easier to have the property adjudicated to be *his* more than *hers*, where the laws don't explicitly state that each party has a legal interest in half the community property.

What about that tax rebate that should reach you any day? Any checks on their way to you are generally treated as though they already existed for the purposes of divvying up, unless they are not to be used in the *immediate* future. Pension rights, for example, may or may not be divided when *you* divide (see Page 77).

Jointly incurred debts? Like assets these are divided too. Who *incurred* the debt is generally less important than who can more easily pay for it.

What actually happens in a divorce proceeding? Is there a big courtroom scene?

The scene varies from state to state, even within a state, depending on whether the couple has children, property, and debts and whether the divorce is actively contested. What's common to *all* states? A full-blown courtroom scene, replete with "Your honor, I object!" represents just a tiny fraction of all divorces filed and granted.

In a strictly no-fault setting, a brief appearance before the judge is usually all that's necessary after the divorce papers have been filed. Why? "No contest" is relevant. Even in a "fault" state like Illinois, many divorces are issued on the basis of default. In other words, if your husband doesn't show up on your court date, you'll be granted the divorce in his *absence*—provided your lawyer can show evidence that he was in fact given notice that the proceedings were taking place and that he failed to respond.

What if you live in a state where more than an allegation is required to show that your marriage is "irretrievably broken" and your spouse contests the divorce? Or *you* determine not to give your husband a divorce? As a practical matter, it's almost impossible to prevent divorce when one party wants it. But this is one situation where a hotly litigated trial might still take place—if the parties can afford the attorneys' fees. Nowadays, however, the divorce is almost always granted.

When child custody or property division can't be peacefully resolved by settlement agreements drafted by his and her lawyers, a court hearing might be necessary. But it's often possible in this case for the divorce to be granted speedily, with a *separate* trial to resolve the contested custody and property issues.

Despite seemingly insurmountable disagreements, husband and wife, in the vast majority of cases, come to a compromise about who gets what. And, once the judge reads through it and is satisfied that it's reasonable, that's that.

What's in such a settlement agreement? Everything—alimony, if it's to be amicably extended; child custody, support, and visitation; and the division of the couple's money and property. Do the dividing couple prepare this list themselves? Not usually. Each spouse tells his or her lawyer what he/she wants and the lawyers battle it out, checking with their respective clients from time to time. You might want to emphasize to your lawyer that no settlement is to be accepted without your prior approval.

How can you louse up your settlement agreement? By becoming so worn down by the entire divorce trauma that, just to be through with the strain, you agree too quickly to terms you haven't fully thought about. And another word of caution: Once you have a lawyer, it's not ethical for your husband's lawyer to call or otherwise contact you. He's to contact your lawyer. Some opposing lawyers will try this tactic to bully (or charm) you into accepting far less than you're due!

What if your husband contacts you directly for a settlement chat?

If you're on good terms, you may want to hear him out. But you do have the option of directing him to your attorney and you should do so if your lawyer has recommended this approach, or if your husband is pressuring you.

And, to preserve your rights, your best bet is to clear *everything* with your lawyer before accepting any offers or relinquishing any property. That's what you're paying her for!

I've heard that California has found a way to circumvent the present system by providing for lawyerless divorces. Is this true?

In certain cases!

The "no-court" divorce doesn't apply to every California couple. It's restricted to couples who have been married less than two years, have no children, and have no substantial property or debts.

If the couple owns a condo, a house, or land, they don't have grounds for the "no-court" procedure. If they have more than $5,000 in personal property, they're still required to go through a court proceeding to safeguard their own interests. At the same time, if the couple, or either one of them, owes more than $2,000 in debts, the "shortcut" divorce isn't available.

These restrictions were established by the California state legislature to sort out couples likely to need the full judicial protection of a "long form" procedure. That leaves couples whose shortcut approach wouldn't be likely to work substantial hardships on each spouse.

The California special still requires the couple to plan for division of property. They must fill out legal forms indicating who gets what and these forms are submitted to the court with a fee, generally $50. After a six-month waiting period, either hubby or wife has the right to go back to court and ask the judge to grant the divorce.

If you're seriously planning a "do-it-yourself" split decision in another state, you might want to contemplate the California guidelines to determine whether you'd qualify for a "short-form" divorce there. If *not*, you may want to rethink before you solo before the judge.

Child Custody

I've heard that fathers are often awarded custody these days, and I'm worried. My husband isn't a good parent! How does a court determine who gets custody when the parents get divorced?

Custody is now awarded on the basis of the "best interests" of the child. But ways of determining "best interests" have undergone some interesting changes over the years.

The law used to require the courts to award custody based on a "presumption in favor of the mother." This was especially true when the child was in his/her "tender years," but the courts routinely viewed all children, all the way up to teen-agers, as still being in their "tender years"!

Right now, only 20 percent of the states still stick to this "tender years doctrine" of awarding children to the mother whenever humanly possible. In fact, the statutes and case law decisions of more than half the states specifically say that the sex of the parent is *not* a factor in custody decisions. And, of the states that still favor the mother, the tender years doctrine has often been modified to apply only to children of *genuinely* tender years.

But now that fathers can be legally considered equally fit to be awarded custody, rumors abound. Perfectly fit mothers are almost routinely denied custody, some fear, because the father can provide a larger home for the kids or because of an anti-woman backlash in the courts. The statistical truth? Mothers are almost routinely awarded custody, even in those states that purport *not* to presume the mother is more fit than the father.

The courts are now freer to explore which parent the children actually feel is the one in the "mothering" or "nurturing" role. If that parent happens to be the mother, as is still so often the case, the courts are very likely to award custody to her. When both husband and wife work outside the home—remember, nearly half of all mothers do—and both share equally in childcare activities, it's sometimes more difficult for the court to figure out who the "psychological mother" is. The parent whose "job" it is to remember the child's shoe size and dental appointments is still the parent more likely to be awarded custody, no matter which parent drives the child to the shoe store, and no matter who foots the bill.

Statistically, men still out-earn women by a significant percentage and, consequently, can afford the bigger backyard, the private school, and the separate bedroom that the court would like to see children enjoy. And it's also true that the child support payments awarded by the court aren't nearly large enough to pay for these creature comforts on the mother's turf, if she's in a lower tax bracket than he is. With this combination behind him, the working father is occasionally able to persuade the court that he can provide higher quality childcare during working hours than the working mother could muster on *her* salary. And, with all other things being equal, finances can become the determining factor. But such situations remain the exceptions, especially when childcare has been left mostly to mom during the child's life.

Once custody has been granted, it takes an extremely serious change in circumstances for the custodial parent to lose the children. The courts are very sensitive to the fact that upheaval itself can be as damaging to children as having them remain in a situation that's less—but not *overwhelmingly* less—than ideal! A drop in income, for example, is rarely a basis for a parent to lose custody once it's been granted. And, generally, the longer a parent has had custody, the more reluctant the court is to interfere with the situation.

I wasn't faithful to my husband. Now that we're divorcing, can my extramarital sex life provide a basis for the court to deny me child custody?

The court can deny you *alimony* payments, in a very few states, as an adulterous wife. But child custody is *not* awarded or denied on the basis of spousal virtue or lack of it, only *parental* virtue. Child custody, as well as financial arrangements for the child's support, aren't a matter of reward to a "good" spouse or punishment to a "bad" one. The "best interests" of the child are still the court's basis for a custody award.

Will the court take into account at all your adulterous relationships? As one factor of many, yes—*if* it can be proved they actually had a damaging effect on your children and the damage continues, so that the children's best interests wouldn't be served by their being in your custody.

Some judges have stated that, unless the conduct of the mother was "outrageous"—performing adulterous acts in front of the children, for example—the issue of adultery itself didn't close the door on the mother's right to custody.

Lesbian and bisexual women, however, have historically lost custody of their children because of discrimination against their sexual preference. Ignoring the fact that the mother's sexual activities were a private matter never viewed by the children, the courts have been ready to accept as evidence of damage to the children the fact that the mother's partners were entertained in the family home! Although there's still no clear-cut body of new law on this point, the situation is changing. As early as 1973, a Michigan court went on record as saying the issue of lesbianism was *not* in itself a determining factor of unfitness for custody and, in 1978, an Illinois court stated that lesbianism was not an issue, but awarded custody to the father.

I'm divorced and have custody of my children. I'm living with a man, but we're not married. Because of my living arrangement, my husband is threatening to try to get custody of the kids. I want to keep custody. Do I have a chance?

Yes!

In 1978, this issue was dealt with by the Illinois Appellate Court. It ruled that a divorced mother was entitled to keep custody of her three daughters even though she was living with a man out of wedlock.

In that case, her ex-husband sought to regain custody of the seven, ten, and twelve-year-olds on the basis that her live-in relationship constituted an "improper moral climate" for them.

And the lower court agreed with the children's father, saying that a change of custody was crucial for the "spiritual well-being and development of the children." But the higher, appellate court nixed that judgment. The appellate court found the mother's relationship with her boyfriend not to be harmful to her daughters. (And all this, by the way, in a state that technically does *not* presume the mother to be the fit parent!)

Three appellate judges heard the case and one stated, "There was no evidence of any fears aroused in the children." Said another: "Whether right or wrong, it appears to be more and more common for a person, including a divorced parent, to live with someone of the opposite sex without marriage." And because of this changing pattern plus growing cultural acceptability, the judge added that it would be difficult to insulate children from live-together life-styles anyway.

But, lest you be moved by this decision to merge kiddies, lover, and you into a common household, be aware that the third judge took exception to those two liberal attitudes. "When a mother teaches her children that her own criminal conduct is proper," he said, "it is unlikely that she will be able to proscribe any future il-legal activities of the children."

Does this decision mean that your living with a man can't be the *sole* basis for your ex-husband to contest custody? Yes, in Illinois and other states with similar decisions.

Does it mean that your ex is legally barred from trying to prove that the kids are, *in fact,* being damaged by your live-in relation-ship? No! Since the best interests of the children are the determin-ing factors in every custody case, the courts may still entertain *evi-dence* that your relationship is harmful to the children.

As cohabitation becomes more customary, more states will doubtlessly rule that, as a practical matter, living together isn't an *automatic* reason for termination of custody. Plus further court deci-sions will undoubtedly define exactly what type of conduct within such a relationship *would* be objectionable—against the best in-terests of the children. Although the whole issue will still be subject to case-by-case scrutiny, it'll then become increasingly possible to predict whether you're jeopardizing your custody rights when you move in with a man. And, incidentally, your alimony award may legally stop when you move in with your male friend, depending upon your state.

Right now, the best that can be said is that, both formally and informally, the courts seem to be facing reality more and more on this point. Whether the laws of *your* state are likely to be as reasonable in *your* situation is still a matter to explore with your lawyer.

My friend's ex-husband didn't return little Michael after a holiday visit to Disneyland. Her lawyer could do very little because the laws weren't sufficiently clear on the subject. Is the issue of "child-snatching" by the noncustodial parent getting some legislative attention?

Yes!

The problem of child-snatching, one parent abducting the child from the other, seldom revealing where the child is or whether he or she is safe, is the subject of several state as well as proposed federal laws. Both criminal and non-criminal laws are being considered and passed to deal with this dilemma.

Now pending in Congress is a bill called the "Uniform Child Custody Jurisdiction Act"—federal legislation requiring the courts of each state to honor and enforce the custody and visitation decrees of every *other* state. Right now, extradition procedures, involving considerable legal and taxpayer expense plus miles of red tape, are often necessary to enforce custody and visitation rights thwarted by out-of-state moves on the part of the "snatching" parent. But, if this bill is passed it would make it impossible for a parent to avoid enforcement of those court-ordered custody/visitation rights by fleeing to another state with the child. It would, in effect, let any state snitch on the snatcher.

Congress isn't alone in such efforts. Individual states are drafting legislation in response to these problems too. A new Illinois bill, for example, makes it a felony for a parent to abduct his or her own child from the rightful custodial parent if the snatcher hides the child in Illinois, or takes the child out-of-state. Other states are passing anti-snatcher laws too.

But still sticky is the problem of child-snatching *after* divorce papers have been filed in court, but *before* the divorce is granted and custody rights are determined! Under these circumstances, the snatcher may not be technically running afoul of the current laws of his or her state, since there has been no judicial determination of the custodial parent, and therefore no determination of that parent's rights! Legal help for the victimized parent and child in this situation is often inadequate under the present laws.

What can you do if you suspect your spouse is distressed enough to abduct your children? When your lawyer files your petition for divorce, he or she can, at the same time, ask the judge for an order preventing your husband from removing the children outside your city or state's jurisdiction until custody is determined.

My husband and I agreed that he should have custody of our child. I make quite a bit more money than he does and I pay $250 a month in child support. I'm entitled to liberal visitation, but my husband refuses to make the child available for visits, despite a court order requiring him to do just that! Am I still required to pay child support?

Probably!

Traditionally, the issues of visitation and child support haven't been legally contingent on each other. If a parent has been denied his or her court-ordered visitation privileges, he or she could bring a court proceeding to compel visitation, but is not allowed to stop paying.

Flipping the coin, a parent who didn't make required child support payments traditionally couldn't be denied visitation on this basis alone. But, as a practical matter, a parent in arrears wouldn't be likely to show up in court to press for visitation, because he or she would find himself or herself being pressed by the court for those missing child support checks.

But, in a recent landmark decision, the Illinois Appellate Court decreed that, under certain circumstances, a parent's obligation to pay child support could be temporarily suspended, or even permanently terminated when the custodial parent continually denies the other parent court-ordered visitation privileges.

Those certain circumstances? In this case, the custodial parent, the mother, had repeatedly denied the father his rights to see their child. Dad went to court again and again; the court again and again issued orders requiring Mom to permit visitation, orders which she ignored. Psychiatric evidence was brought up in the case showing that the mother's conduct was indeed destroying the relationship between father and son. But an important factor in the court's decision was that termination of support would be no hardship on the child. The mother had sufficient income to support the child herself, the court said, and relieved the father of his financial obligation.

The father of my children hasn't sent me a dime of the child support the judge ordered him to pay. I can't even take him to court, because I don't know where to find him. I don't like being on welfare, but I can't get work. Are there laws to help?

Yes!

A child-support enforcement program, sponsored by the federal and state governments, helps collect over $1 billion a year by tracing parents who have skipped out on child-support duties and taking them to court. Why such efficiency on the part of the government? Somebody has to pay. If dad won't and mom can't, Uncle Sam has to write the checks. If the children's parents are indigent, that's exactly why financial aid to families with dependent children exists. But when one parent is indigent and the other is in hiding, gainfully employed but shirking child-care responsibilities, it's a different matter.

The new program has a start toward success: About 600,000 welfare families and 400,000 non-welfare families are now receiving the support payments the court had ordered from previously non-paying parents.

If your spouse is $5,000 in arrears in court-ordered child support and the state collects it from him, do *you* get the money? It depends. If you've had to go on welfare because of the skipped payments, the state is allowed to use the money to reimburse itself for your welfare payments. And the federal government gets some too, since it's been carrying about half the state's welfare bills. But subsequent payments made to you by the father are generally yours to keep.

What if you weren't on welfare and requested your state's "child-dodger" agency to help you get the support payments the court ordered the father to pay? You and the kids get every penny the government collects, minus a small service charge.

If you've applied for welfare, chances are you've been advised of the "child-dodger" laws. If you're not on welfare and want to use the locator service, your local attorney general or regional department of Health, Education, and Welfare can direct you to the new Office of Child Support Enforcement.

I'm about to marry a wonderful guy and my daughter already calls him "Daddy." He'd like to adopt her, but her biological father, whom I never married, absolutely refuses to consent. Can he block her chance for a two-parent home?

It depends on how parental *he's* been!

In a landmark decision, the U.S. Supreme Court recently permitted a mother's new husband to adopt her child, despite the protests of the child's natural father.

Why? Although the natural father had never been declared an unfit parent, he'd never married the mother and hadn't taken significant responsibility for the care, education, and feeding of his offspring. True, he visited the child frequently, but had never made his home with the mother and child.

These factors persuaded the Supreme Court that the Georgia state law requiring the natural father's consent was too onerous and they struck it down, a none-too-subtle tip for other states to re-write their laws on this point accordingly!

What was the Supreme Court's "bottom line?" You guessed it—the "best interests of the child!" Did the law shut out illegitimate fathers altogether? No. They're still entitled to notice and a chance for a fair hearing before a new daddy steps in. But now, their veto may be overriden *if* they haven't really parented. Your own lawyer can review the facts of your situation and advise you of your child's chances to live like the Waltons.

Abortion

I'm in the first trimester of my pregnancy and I intend to have an abortion. My doctor concurs in my decision. May the state interfere with my right to do so?

No!

According to the Supreme Court, if you're in your first trimester, the decision is between you and your doctor. Where you choose to have the procedure done, in a private clinic, in your gynecologist's office, or in a hospital, is up to you. But, because the Supreme Court specified mutual decision-making responsibility, the state is probably entitled to require that you have a doctor perform the abortion.

Can a state overreact in this requirement? Ask Marla Pitchford, victim of a Kentucky law prohibiting anyone but a physician from performing the operation. Six months pregnant and desperate, Pitchford gave herself an abortion by inserting a knitting needle through her cervix into the uterus. Shortly after she sought follow-up medical attention, Pitchford was arrested and stood trial, with a possible twenty-year sentence looming ahead of her.

Reluctantly, Pitchford's attorney determined that she had a basis for pleading not guilty by reason of insanity and on that basis, Pitchford was acquitted and released. "It is the first time in the history of the nation," said Pitchford's lawyer, Flora Templeton Stuart, "that a woman was tried for aborting herself."

However, the trial never actually tested the state's law. While the first priority, rightfully, was to have Pitchford found not guilty, the basis for acquittal does *not* serve as a precedent indicating that a law like Kentucky's is unconstitutional, because the issue was never addressed. In fairness to Kentucky, the statute was probably intended to protect women from quacks and back-alley butchers. But it ended up harassing Pitchford, and could do the same for others in her plight. Nevertheless, the statute still stands.

Despite the U.S. Supreme Court's favorable stance on abortion, states themselves often put up their own unlawful hurdles to inter-

fere with abortion procedures during even the first trimester. How?
They propose, and pass, laws and ordinances requiring abortion
clinics to be licensed only after meeting far more stringent conditions than are required of any other kind of medical clinic. They
have required "informed consent"—whereby the patient is forced to
view pictures of embryo development. (Compare that to a tonsilec-
tomy. A patient is never required to look at slides of her tonsils
before they're removed.) And they have required spousal consent
before the procedure is performed. These restrictions are repeatedly
struck down in the courts as being unconstitutional in view of the
Supreme Court decision. But taking even the most blatantly unconstitutional legislation to court is a costly and time-consuming process; therefore, much of it stays on the books long enough to make it
more difficult to get an abortion than it should be.

And Congress does its part too in trying to sneak past the Supreme Court rulings. The favorite method is to attach anti-abortion
riders—additions to proposed bills—to completely unrelated legislation. The idea is to let a controversial bit of legislation ride on the
coattails of a bill known to be so popularly approved that the whole
thing will just sail through and become law.

But it doesn't always work. For example, in August 1978 a constitutional amendment was pending in the Senate that would give
the District of Columbia voting representation in Congress—a goal
that most people believed was worthwhile. But to *that* amendment,
Senator William Scott (Republican from Virginia) added the following amendment: "The power to regulate the circumstances under
which pregnancy may or may not be terminated is reserved to the
respective states and territories of the U.S." Of the sixty-seven
senators voting, eighteen were in favor of the abortion amendment.
Of those who voted against it, many said they actually agreed with
it, but didn't feel that it should be combined with the Washington,
D.C. issue. And so the whole thing was tabled.

*What if I choose to have my abortion during the second trimester? Can the
state regulate that?*

Yes!

The state can—and most states do—have legislation requiring that second trimester abortions be performed under specified medical conditions. All these laws were passed to ensure the safety of the patient, since abortion during the second trimester is a more difficult medical procedure than in the first trimester.

Can my husband get an injunction to prevent me from having an abortion?

No!

The U.S. Supreme Court has determined that it is the constitutional right of a woman to have an abortion. So the choice is the woman's personal decision. According to the law, a woman's husband cannot compel her to continue her pregnancy because of his beliefs, his desire for a child, or for any other reason.

Is my husband's consent necessary for me to get an abortion?

No.

Every now and then, a state will pass legislation requiring the husband's consent to a routine first or second trimester abortion. But this legislation repeatedly gets defeated in the courts on constitutional grounds.

Does a minor have the right to an abortion too?

Probably!

The Supreme Court has held that minors have the constitutional right both to obtain contraceptives *and* to have abortions without the knowledge or consent of their parents.

The precedent was set when the U.S. Supreme Court struck down a Missouri state statute that had required unmarried girls under eighteen to secure parental consent as a condition for having an abortion. States that have such restrictions argue that they're not unconstitutional. They're needed, the states say, to strengthen the family as a social institution and to safeguard the child-rearing rights of parents. But the U.S. Supreme Court agreed with minor girls who argued that those state restrictions do *not* legitimately serve their intended goals.

In a recent Illinois decision, the court noted that the pregnancy of a minor daughter had caused a serious rift in the family to begin with. And the Court pointed out that parental power to block her abortion decision could hardly be expected to restore the family to a happy, peaceful state.

The Illinois law like the Missouri law was struck down by federal courts as being unconstitutional. In this case, the law had required unmarried girls under eighteen to get parental or *court* consent for an abortion. In other words, if her parents said no, the girl could try and get the court to say yes. And that law presumes of course that the average teen-age girl first of all knows how to *find* the federal court, then knows how to bring a petition up for a court review!

The suit against the Illinois law was brought by the American Civil Liberties Union on behalf of two unmarried seventeen-year-olds and four Chicago physicians. The ACLU argued that the Illinois statute deprived the girls and their doctors of their constitutional right to privacy.

Said the Illinois court, while parents "generally should be informed" about their daughters' decision to have an abortion, the girls can't be forced to tell their parents because "it may not be in the minor's best interest to have her parents informed of her condition in all cases." The court also said that the law was forcing a girl into an ordeal "at a time when she is experiencing the most physically and psychologically critical period of her life." In addition, the court concluded that singling out *unmarried* girls for special requirements was discriminatory.

Some restrictions on minors' access to abortion may ultimately be judged in the U.S. Supreme Court as being constitutional, but they haven't as yet. As the court pointed out in the Illinois law situation, a statute that intends to pass constitutional muster "must be drafted in a way to aid the minor by easing her burdens rather than adding to them."

What can a minor do if her doctor or an abortion clinic refuses to perform her abortion?

If they say they won't take care of you without parental or court consent, here's where to turn for help. Call the National Abortion Rights Action League in Washington, D.C., or one of their regional offices in your city. Check the phone directory for listings in your city of the American Civil Liberties Union, Planned Parenthood, your area's legal assistance foundation, legal aid, the National Organization of Women, or any other feminist organization in your community. All of them are likely to come to your aid.

Is it legal for "anti-choice" groups to picket abortion clinics?

Yes! But *lawful* protests must *not* interfere with the operation of the clinic or with patients going in and out.

If patients on their way in or out of an abortion clinic are harassed, they can take the matter to a lawyer for a determination on whether court action is warranted. A priest was successfully sued for "intentional infliction of emotional distress" as a result of his outrageous behavior toward a patient leaving an abortion clinic. The court found his actions to be above and beyond his rights of freedom of speech to the point of deliberate cruelty.

There are indeed horror stories. In Cleveland recently, an anti-choice demonstrator practiced his first amendment right of free expression, by throwing into the face of a clinic technician a chemical that blinded her for several hours. The demonstrator then poured gasoline around the clinic lab and lit it. The staff and twenty patients managed to flee to safety, but the entire clinic was destroyed in the fire.

In Cincinnati, another abortion clinic was bombed with an acid reportedly on the government's list of chemical warfare agents. In Virginia, demonstrators kicked a clinic staff member who was six and one-half months pregnant at the time. In St. Paul, Minnesota, an entire Planned Parenthood clinic was destroyed by arson and later bullets were fired into the building. The National Abortion Rights

Action League reports that kidnap and death threats have been made by anti-choice groups against children of the Planned Parenthood board members.

Is anything being done about this terrorism? At least in one case, yes. In June 1978, a federal district court judge in Virginia issued a permanent injunction against anti-abortion trespassers; they had repeatedly exceeded by legions the bounds of their first amendment rights in their hostile protest at the Northern Virginia Women's Medical Center in Fairfax County.

Even though the demonstrators had broken into the clinic, photographed and harassed the patients, taken over the clinic telephones, and done other damage, state court judges had dismissed various trespass charges against them. Finally, represented by the American Civil Liberties Union, the clinic and its patients brought suit. And the injunction was issued.

The injunction does not bar *peaceful* demonstrations. But it *does* bar the use of criminal trespass and terrorist tactics against persons who are exercising their constitutional rights to have abortions and to perform them.

Wills

I don't have a will, but I'd want my husband to inherit all my property anyway. Isn't that what automatically happens if I die without a will?

No!

A person who dies without a will is said to die "intestate." The laws of each state differ with regard to how the property of one who dies intestate gets distributed. But, in general, the laws of *most* states would allot from one-half to one-third of your property to your husband, with the rest equally divided among your children. What if you have no children? Your parents, grandparents, siblings, even your nieces and nephews may have rights to the bulk of your worldly goods and the law just doesn't care that you've always hated your twin sister. She, too, gets a crack at the heirloom china and more.

What if your husband dies before you and leaves no will? The same thing happens. You're entitled to your "statutory share," the amount the statute, or law, of your state has established for the surviving spouse of one who dies intestate. If you have children, the bulk of the assets—minimally, two-thirds to one-half—will be divided equally among them, in most states. But in some states, the surviving spouse, be it husband *or* wife, gets a "widow's share" equal to the share each child gets.

In those states, the percentage she receives would depend on the number of children. Say a woman's husband left property valued at $200,000, and the couple had four children. Then, the widow and each child would be entitled to one-fifth or $40,000 (minus various taxes, of course). And because it takes a *will* to name a guardian of children's property, the widow will not necessarily be legally entitled to guide the children in planning or spending their own shares of the estate.

How formal must a will be? I don't intend to scribble one onto a cocktail napkin, but can I just type out a list of my property, name who's to collect what, and then sign it?

Generally not!

The degree of formality depends, once again, on the laws of your own state. In general, your act of signing a will must be witnessed. But not every state acknowledges your spouse as a proper witness; some states require more than one witness.

State laws vary as to how definitively you're required to describe your property. "Everything I own" may not be sufficient; "the jewelry in my safe deposit box" may not be sufficient; even "all my stock" may not be sufficient! On the other hand, you're probably not required to explain that you're "bequeathing to my loving cousin Martha my five-by-two-by-one and one-half-inch tortoise-shell cigarette case with the inlaid rhinestone flamingo and the 'Viva Las Vegas' inscription on the inside cover." The laws of your state, like most states, lie somewhere in between, but you need to know exactly where.

Plus, states vary in the legal adequacy of the way you phrase bequests of "after-acquired" property. That's the goodies and dollars you take in *after* making your will, and which you can't describe now, because how did you know you'd win the lottery? Chances are, you have miles to go before you sleep, and your thoughtful "and everything I may earn in the future to my little daughter Jennifer" may leave not-so-little Jennifer *without* the bankroll you earned and intended her to have.

It's your best bet to consult a lawyer familiar with the laws of your state when it comes to wills. Because, if your will is considered legally "defective," your property will be divided as if you had never made one.

After years of hard work, I earned my M.B.A. and command a good salary. My husband has never been particularly supportive of either my schooling or my work. Can I disinherit him and leave all my money to a woman's scholarship fund?

No!

You can have a will leaving him nothing, or one bestowing your old tennis shoes to him as a token of appreciation for his support. But, in either case, he has the right to renounce the will and to inherit the amount he *would* have inherited had you died without one—usually, one-third to one-half of your property.

The reverse is true, too. He can threaten to cut you out of his will, but you *can't* wind up with less than the amount you'd be entitled to if he died intestate. Renouncing this kind of will is fairly routine. The laws are well established on the rights of the widow or widower to renounce.

If you live in a community property state—Arizona, California, Idaho, Louisiana, Nevada, New Mexico, Texas, or Washington—husband and wife are each legally presumed, with certain exceptions, to own half of *everything*. The exceptions: If your husband had property which he owned before he married you, or if he inherited property at any time after he married you, most community property laws do *not* give you the right to that money up the middle. But otherwise, in those states, when your spouse dies, with or without a will, half of all the family property remains *yours* and your inheritance concerns disposition of *his* half.

In the other forty-two non-community property states, you don't go automatic "halvsies" with your mate. So the need for both you *and* your spouse to have wills is literally twice as important!

But I have children by a previous marriage and I want to leave everything to them! Can't my will take care of this?

No!

Again, a surviving spouse who's been omitted from his mate's will has the legal right to declare the will invalid and to inherit whatever amount would have been his or hers, just as if there had been no will. This unique right—available *only* to the widow or widower and *not* to any other relative—is meant to be a safeguard for the surviving spouse. (There are some exceptions in Louisiana, a state that doesn't allow children to be completely disinherited.)

No matter how virtuous your motives may be in not willing anything to your surviving spouse—he was a rat, your children need the money and he doesn't need a cent, or you want to leave it all to charity—your spouse can collect his or her "statutory" share of the estate. ("Estate," by the way, doesn't have to mean a forty-room mansion on fifty acres, including polo grounds. It's just legalese for whatever money, property, and other goodies you leave when you die.)

If you have children by a previous husband or friend and you don't want your present husband to get his hands on your money when you depart, a marriage contract drawn up by your lawyer *before* the wedding can help in some states. It's generally more difficult for this type of contract to be enforced if it's entered into *after* you've said "I do."

Your lawyer can advise you about other ways of transferring all your money for your children or whomever the inheritors will be— into trusts, for example, or bonds—so that the money or property isn't officially part of your estate.

The law isn't always in keeping with common sense and you may very well find property you assumed you'd given to your kids coming right back into your estate on a technicality. For example, if you put $10,000 in a savings account in your daughter's name, it's *hers*, or is it? It may depend on whether *you* can make withdrawals, even if you're taking the money out for *her* racquetball lessons.

My partner and I own a boutique. If she dies before I do, is there a law that lets me automatically inherit the whole boutique?

No!

If you're in business with another person, it's crucial that you have a written partnership agreement (1) stating that the business is to continue if either of you should die and (2) making reasonable arrangements for the survivor to buy out the interests of the deceased partner from her estate. If there *isn't* a written partnership agreement, the laws of your state may automatically terminate the partnership, leaving your deceased partner's heirs with the right to liquidate your business for "their" share!

What if you and your friend never really discussed the *nature* of your business relationship. The boutique just sort of evolved out of a project you started together and you really don't think of yourselves as partners? In this case, the laws of most states generally provide that, if it looked to the public as if you were partners, then you are! And, should one of you die, the legal problems of not having planned by contract in advance are exactly the same as if you'd been contractual partners, but without a partnership agreement to guard the survivor's part of the business!

The same types of agreements are also important if you have a "closely held" or very small corporation, with only two, or, at any rate, very few, shareholders.

And contracts like that aren't important only if you're in business with a friend. If your husband's your partner in business as well as marriage, it's also essential to make provisions for the continued operation of the business after the death of one or divorce.

Years ago, my husband and I got a terrific deal on two hundred acres of undeveloped property. Now, the property is worth ten times what we paid for it! The land is in both our names, so what will happen to it if my husband dies?

It depends!

When you say it's in both your names, the *specific* kind of co-ownership makes a big difference. Is the land in joint tenancy, or is it held by both of you as tenants in common?

If joint tenancy is your answer, then both of you have a half ownership in *all* the land. In other words, you can't point to "his" and "her" acres. Both of you equally own each and every one of them! In this situation, if one of you dies, the other gets the *entire* two-hundred-acre piece of land.

However, depending on the value of the property at the time of the co-owner's death, plus certain other factors, there can be serious tax problems. Unless the widow (or widower) can *prove* she/he contributed to the purchase price of the property, the land could very well be subject to very heavy taxation. This places an unfair burden on the widow in some states. Why? The money she used toward the purchase price may not always be legally viewed as "hers"; it could be viewed as her husband's! Historically, women who co-owned farms (and businesses) with their husbands were hit especially hard by these discriminatory laws. Recently, however, federal, and some state, laws have changed to ease the widow's unfair tax burdens, and more changes are likely to follow.

Don't think, though, that putting land or other property in joint tenancy will substitute for a will. It won't. A will can help you avoid some of these tax problems.

Now, if your property is owned by tenancy in common rather than joint tenancy, the two halves *can* be divided at the time of death or divorce. In this situation, whether you inherit your husband's half depends on his will or the intestacy laws of your state.

Land held this way can turn out to be pretty rough terrain. If no will was made, then part of your husband's half may go to *others*, according to state laws. For example, you and your husband may have believed that those green acres would automatically become all yours upon his death. But, in fact, his children by another marriage, and although rarely, his other relatives, might have rights to at least part of his half of the property. In addition, they might even be able to go to court to force the sale of *all* the property, meaning your half, too!

What happens when it's not all in the family? If you're buying land with someone who's not related to you, make especially certain that each of you has a will reflecting your mutual understanding about what will become of the land or its cash value if either of you should die.

How about jointly-held securities? Can these become mine if my husband dies without a will?

Yes, but...

Your problems will be the same as if you owned real estate in joint tenancy. If your husband dies, with or without a will, *you* may be required to pay federal estate tax on your *own* stocks, bonds, and mutual funds, unless you can prove that the money used to buy them was *yours*. And what money qualifies as "yours"? The federal government will look to the laws of your state to figure that out.

Unfortunately, many states do not regard money your husband earned but shared with you as "yours." And a few states—believe it or not—don't recognize money you earned *yourself* as "yours," unless you keep it in a separate bank account or take other steps the state requires as proof!

However, even if the money used to purchase the securities came from your husband's paycheck, you won't usually have this problem *if* the securities are in your own name.

This sticky dilemma also applies to joint savings accounts. When your husband dies, you may be forced to pay federal estate taxes on all the money in the account because your home state has an archaic view of a married woman's right to money.

Here again, a lawyer can help you plan your estate *before* you find yourself the victim of this kind of sex discrimination.

2

On the Job

Employment Rights

What kind of sexist practices are really illegal?

The list is virtually endless now and it keeps growing as the proportion of women in the workforce increases! You're undoubtedly aware of the "old standards," and, yes, they keep being sung by employer after employer until a lawsuit changes his tune! Does this mean that, once the court has said one employer's policy is illegal, all employers will change their policies to conform with the court's ruling? Hardly! But the more times the court rules against a specific form of sexism the easier it is to win your case involving the same form of sexism. In fact, it's in this type of situation that your chances of a quick, fair settlement out-of-court are most likely.

On the list of illegalities are refusing to hire women; refusing to promote women, or to give them seniority in the same situation where a man would be entitled to it; refusing to pay women the same as men; giving only women the lowest-paying shifts or the lowest-paying factory or sales jobs; refusing to admit qualified women into management training programs; refusing to let wom-

39

en have assignments that require travel; giving women editors and writers mostly "traditional" subjects to write about, such as fashion or society parties; height requirements that exclude most women; pregnancy discrimination. You name it!

When is an excuse *no* excuse? When an employer or potential employer says, "I'm not discriminating against you because you're a woman, only because you (check one) have young children, are married and might get pregnant."

There are practices that still fall into the murky gray area—they're not quite kosher, but they're not strictly illegal, either. Having a secretary make coffee or do other personal tasks, for example, detracts from the fact that the secretary is an office worker, not a spouse or a maid. And, right now, a secretary has no *right* to be paid on a level with a non-secretarial worker, male or female, unless she can prove her duties are the same as, or almost the same as, that person's.

But, nevertheless, things are changing, especially in government jobs, where some degree of affirmative action is required. And, coming around, too, but more slowly, are companies that have government contracts of $10,000 or more (see Page 42).

Yes, the law *is* evolving to the point where eventual upgrading of the secretarial position—including a higher pay scale—is a real possibility.

But does this suggest that, now, if the vast percentage of females employed by a company are secretaries, discrimination can't be proved? No! This *is* one of the standard symptoms the courts look at in deciding whether women are being unlawfully denied access to employment opportunities. What's generally *not* presently required is that the same women now in those secretarial spots be elevated to management.

If I think I'm being discriminated against in employment because of my sex, what laws can help me?

The main one is the wide-reaching federal law, Title VII of the Civil

Rights Act of 1964. It prohibits most kinds of employment discrimination based on sex as well as race.

Plus, a good percentage of the states—and even cities—have additional laws preventing unfair employment practices. Many laws overlap with Title VII, but sometimes they offer extra protections.

By virtue of the equal protection requirement, the U.S. Constitution can be helpful if you're discriminated against by the government, or even in places, such as schools, that have extensive government funding.

Some states have state constitutional provisions much broader than the U.S. Constitution. Illinois, for example, has a state constitution that prohibits discrimination in employment, public *or* private. Feminist attorney Maureen J. McGann was successful in establishing that the Illinois provision meant just what it said when a woman was denied a job at an accounting firm because the personnel department told her they were looking for a "fellow." Yes, Title VII would have brought about the same results, as would Illinois' state fair employment practices act. But the Illinois constitution enabled the accountant to go into state court quickly, bypassing a few miles of bureaucratic red tape.

If you work for a company with even a small government contract, you're entitled to fair treatment under the U.S. Department of Labor's Office of Federal Contract Compliance (OFCC).

And, if you're a teacher, federal law Title IX prohibits discrimination. There are also executive orders prohibiting employment discrimination against women and minorities. And don't overlook related laws, such as those prohibiting age discrimination.

I work in a law firm with fifteen employees. My boss says he's not required to follow the federal law preventing sex discrimination. I say he is! What does Title VII say?

It depends!

Law firms, doctor's offices, and other professional employers are not exempt from Title VII. Like factories, stores, and the federal government itself, they must comply. There are very few types of employment, in fact, not covered by Title VII.

The number of people that must be employed at a work place before Title VII can be applied is fifteen. Partners or owners aren't employees though; so they are *not* part of the final tally. If your count of fifteen *doesn't* include the boss or other partners, Title VII probably applies.

Can part-time employees count toward lucky fifteen? Yes, if they work regularly during a twenty-week period.

When I applied for work recently, the personnel department tried to channel me into a clerical spot. I think I'm qualified for a higher-paying job, but how do I find out what kinds of positions might be available? Is an employer required to recruit or to post job listings so that I can learn about openings in other departments outside the secretarial grapevine?

Generally a private employer is *not obligated* to recruit. But, if he recruits he's *not entitled* to use only recruitment procedures like word-of-mouth or the "old boys' network" that could automatically exclude women.

Likewise a private employer is *not* generally required to post job openings which might include attractive positions so that current employees might apply for higher-level work. Some unions have pressured employers for this service. And the working women's organizations, such as Boston's 9-5 and Chicago's Women Employed, have had success in putting the squeeze on larger companies to do the same.

Government jobs generally *are* required to be made known. Private employers of course still have the prerogative of *not* publicly announcing jobs. The exception: If your employer has a government contract to provide as little as $10,000 worth of goods or services of any kind, your employer is held to strict standards of nondiscriminatory practices. In fact, this is one of the very few situations in which a private company can be required to engage in affirmative action in promoting and hiring. Who gets government contracts? The list is endless. If your company has been engaged, for example, to plant bushes around a federal building or to sell office supplies of any kind to any federal government agency, it probably has a government contract. And your employer may be obligated to recruit, hire, and promote qualified women and minorities according to a certain timetable.

Banks for example have recently been hit by women who've been unfairly denied access to jobs. Why? They hold *federal* deposits—a government contract in excess of $10,000! Consequently, affirmative action recruitment is a must.

If you have a gripe, who'll process it? The government contract situation is enforced by the U.S. Department of Labor through its Office of Federal Contract Compliance (OFCC). If OFCC agrees that your complaint is warranted, your employer can lose its federal contract unless it hires and promotes a reasonable number of women and minorities!

I know I'm entitled to equal pay for equal work. But what if my job title is different from the man who does the same thing but is paid more than I am, or has a few different job duties?

Equal is as equal does!

In this situation, what's important is *not* who's *listed* as what in the company phone extension directory, but who *does* what! If the duties are generally equivalent, despite the fact that they're not identical, you may well prove discrimination.

Whom to contact with an equal pay complaint? The answer used to be the U.S. Department of Labor, but now it's EEOC! This recent re-routing may cause a bit of procedural confusion for the next year or so but hang in there!

I'm pregnant and in good health. I plan to work up to my due date, then to return to work shortly after. My employer seems to think that pregnancy automatically means long absences, even incompetency! Can I be fired simply because I'm pregnant?

Generally not, unless your employer can prove to EEOC and the other enforcement agencies, that there's a *genuine* danger to you, the fetus, or the public if you continue to work. Airlines for example have been able to persuade EEOC that passenger safety is at stake when a pregnant flight attendant runs the ship. But they generally must provide some *comparable* work for her during the pregnancy—ground duty, for example. And postpartum the worker must be given her old job back, posthaste!

Because of the Occupational Safety and Health Act (OSHA), if you're handling noxious chemicals suspected of producing fetal abnormalities, your company may reassign you but *not* fire you. Reassignment to significantly lower-paying work may lead you to EEOC's doorstep with your bundle of joy in one arm and your sex discrimination complaint in the other!

What if you're *unable* to do your job because of complications related to your condition? You're entitled to whatever sick leave you'd ordinarily have coming if you were out with the flu or anything else and you're entitled to take your accumulated vacation time as well. While government employees have fairly liberal maternity leave guaranteed them, it's still the private employer's prerogative to discharge a woman for taking off more days than company policy allows. And a private company is *not* generally required to provide specific maternity—or paternity—leave. The exception: If it looks as though a particular company is being inflexible and firing women routinely for taking what would seem to be reasonable sick leave to deliver and recover. This discriminatory pattern might be viewed as an illegal employment practice. And private companies with government contracts may also be held to fairer treatment of mothers-to-be.

What if you're perfectly able to keep working late in your pregnancy, even though your company policy says you must leave at the start of your last trimester? It's almost always illegal for an employer to have an arbitrary maternity leave policy, one that doesn't take an individual woman's abilities into account. If your job requires you to leave work after your seventh month, for example, and not to return until the baby is three weeks old, your boss isn't considering *your* situation and you're entitled to complain!

The rights of pregnant workers are expanding, thanks to brand-new legislation which emphasizes that Title VII extends to pregnancy and pregnancy-related conditions. The new law clearly makes discrimination against pregnant workers illegal, and should bring about exciting new advancements as women seek to enforce their new rights under the federal statute.

My union representative just negotiated a new contract for us. I noticed that there was no provision in it to prohibit discrimination on the basis of sex. Also, there are things in the contract that seem to me to allow the employer to job-classify women in sex-discriminatory ways. What are my rights?

You may have a union suit!

Your union must represent females as well as males and EEOC has found unions liable for giving in to discriminatory contracts.

In addition, if your union doesn't take seriously women's grievances against management but eagerly holds the banner high for *male* members, you're entitled to complain to both EEOC and the National Labor Relations Board.

Not only are unions not allowed to sell you out in dealings with management, they're also obligated to make referrals from hiring halls in a nondiscriminatory way.

I'm being harassed on my job not strictly because I'm a woman, but because I'm gay. Does Title VII apply?

No, but you may have rights under other laws!

The laws of a few states—California, for example—are changing to make discrimination against gays an unfair employment practice. Contact your state's commission on unfair employment practices for more information.

Other states—even cities—have very strong commissions on human relations, and they've sometimes helped enact various legal ordinances that could apply to your situation. But right now your chances aren't very encouraging.

Some gays have found recourse through their unions, not because the union contract protected gays, but because it prohibited management from harassing *any* employee!

I'm a teacher. Are there special *laws prohibiting discrimination against me?*

Yes!

"No person in the United States shall, on the basis of sex, be excluded from participation in, be denied the benefits of, or be subjected to discrimination under any program or activity receiving federal financial assistance," according to Title IX of the Educational Amendments of 1972 and under this act numerous regulations have been declared by the Department of Health, Education, and Welfare (HEW).

What specific issues do those generalities cover? Standards of employment, recruitment, compensation, job classification and structure, fringe benefits, marital and parental status, advertising of the job, and pre-employment inquiries are some of the major ones where sex discrimination gets an automatic *F*.

One of the most common areas for a teacher to get a workout in discriminatory practices is athletics. Male coaches are usually paid substantial salaries for their work with high school and college teams. Women coaches, on the other hand, are often paid *nothing* for comparable work. Several actions have been brought under Title IX to even the score.

To seek redress under Title IX, HEW is the agency to contact, but don't expect surefire success. Title IX has proved disappointing in protecting female faculty from discrimination. For example, while the law provides that *serious* discrimination in education can result in the revocation of a school's federal funding, HEW has *never* so much as held the necessary hearing to revoke such funds, *despite* evidence of sex discrimination. The lesson for the teacher: Here's an area where a private lawsuit may be more helpful than seeking redress through the government agency charged with enforcing the law.

However, things may be improving. Thanks to recent lawsuits filed by Women's Equity Action League (WEAL) and other civil rights organizations, HEW is now under court order to enforce Title IX. During the lawsuit, WEAL exposed the fact that, not only had HEW been shirking its Title IX duties, it had actually returned millions of unspent dollars to the government—dollars which were to have gone toward enforcing the equal employment rights of women teachers!

Employment Remedies

What are my procedural rights if I suspect that my employer, union, or an employment agency has violated my rights under Title VII, the broadest of the federal antidiscrimination laws?

You're entitled to file a complaint with the Equal Employment Opportunity Commission (EEOC). It's the massive federal agency whose only job is to enforce Title VII, the most all-encompassing statute in the sex (and race) discrimination area.

If you even *suspect* you're being discriminated against in an employment, union, or pre-employment setting, and you see little hope of a peaceful resolution of the problem, you qualify under EEOC guidelines for filing a complaint.

Filing a complaint is also called "filing a charge," so, after filing that complaint, you're known as a "charging party." That sounds like a fun-loving bullfighter with knowledge of her credit rights, but it's just agency jargon for the employee—or would-be employee—with a beef!

Is it really that easy? Yes and no. First of all, you technically have a little less than six months after the wrong occurred to file with EEOC. But your wording can make a difference. If you allege that the employer, union, or employment agency's discrimination is "ongoing and continuing," you're not bound into a narrow time frame in many cases.

A frequent source of confusion: If yours is one of many states with a fair employment practices agency, federal law requires that your *state* take the first crack at solving your problem. Kafkaesque timetables have spun out as a result of that stipulation. To cut short the time factor, the best route is to file your complaint with both the federal (EEOC) and state agencies *simultaneously*.

When you charge, you have a choice. You're entitled to file your state and EEOC complaint on your own behalf, or on the behalf of yourself *and* others whom you believe to be victims of the same or related discriminatory practices. Both the federal and state enforcement agencies have personnel who will help you describe the discriminatory conduct.

Is a lawyer helpful here? Yes! Because this is one more area where wording can make or break your case. Under the law certain specific elements must be alleged, or EEOC (or the analogous state agency) may have to toss out your complaint for "failure to make a claim."

If you can't afford legal counsel to help you wade and word your way through, many working women's groups can give you accurate and complete information about your employment rights and the procedures involved in filing charges. They can also send one of their members to accompany you to state employment practice enforcement agencies and to your regional EEOC. No, they can't, and won't, practice law or give legal advice. But these groups meet with lawyers and often have up-to-the-minute information about your rights in general.

I suspected I was discriminated against in an employment setting, so I filed a complaint with EEOC. What happens next?

Your employer is notified of the complaint.

Federal laws require EEOC to begin its investigation of your charges and to decide whether there's reasonable cause to believe that an unfair employment practice has taken place within *four months* of the date you filed. But don't hold your breath. Due to an EEOC backlog of as much as three years, the four-month rule just isn't possible to comply with any more. (The back-up gives you some idea, by the way, of how much discrimination may still be going on out there!) Consequently, in order to hasten settlement, EEOC, in three model cities—Chicago, Baltimore, and Dallas— is experimenting with an informal fact-finding hearing scheduled almost immediately after a suit is filed. (For more details, see Page 51.)

If EEOC *does* find substantial evidence of illegality, it will try to eliminate the discrimination through informal conferences. Your employer will be urged to change his tune and perhaps make a cash award; you'll be urged to accept the compromise. At this point you might want to call in your attorney again to set out the facts of your story in an "actionable way," and to help you decide whether you'd be better off accepting a settlement or come out ahead in court.

EEOC encourages voluntary, out-of-court resolution of disputes. But what if no settlement can be reached? The EEOC may bring a lawsuit in federal court on your behalf or on behalf of a class of similarly situated women, whose problems with the employer, union, or employment agency are much the same. Prepare to be in company if the EEOC files suit. No matter how legitimate her individual complaint, rarely does EEOC file such a lawsuit on behalf of just one woman. Instead, EEOC prefers to concentrate its limited personnel and financial resources on areas in which there are a number of complaints against one particular union or company. Because it helps wipe out discrimination on a grand scale, this is called systemic litigation—it sees that the large employer's system of discrimination is abolished. And by the way when EEOC brings the suit, you don't pay their attorney's fees.

What if EEOC won't bring your case to federal court? In this situation, you're entitled to request a "right-to-sue" letter from EEOC so that you can bring the lawsuit yourself, with your own lawyer, not EEOC's, presenting the case. Since you'll require an attorney, this is obviously the costlier alternative. But, some lawyers will represent you on a contingency basis, which means that they'll get a percentage of your winnings but they'll get nothing if you lose.

Once you get that letter, watch your calendar! You *must* file your Title VII lawsuit in federal court within ninety days after your right-to-sue letter is issued, or you give up your right to bring suit!

I've been the victim of employment discrimination under Title VII, but I don't live in one of EEOC's model, fast-action regions. I don't want to wait months or years for EEOC to investigate my case. Can my lawyer bring my Title VII suit in federal court without my going through EEOC first?

No!

Right now, a right-to-sue letter from EEOC is the prerequisite for filing a lawsuit based on Title VII. However, EEOC will routinely issue the letter. This letter is merely an acknowledgment from EEOC that you have "exhausted your administrative remedies." That is, the law requires EEOC to review your gripe before you go to court. But is does *not* prevent you from suing in court even if EEOC thinks you have no valid case! And, as EEOC may not always predict correctly, you may have more success in the courts.

And you are entitled to sue under other laws protecting you from employment discrimination, laws available to you in addition to Title VII.

Your lawyer may encourage you to keep your EEOC complaint pending even while your state or federal lawsuit, under other laws, is pending. If EEOC issues your right-to-sue letter before your other suit is decided by the judge (possible, because most lawsuits take a long time before they're heard), you may often have the right to add your Title VII complaint to the lawsuit already pending.

In this kind of situation, will you be entitled to relief under *all* the different laws that apply? Except for the instances when you're entitled to punitive damages and attorney's fees and costs, the general rule with all—not just sex discrimination—litigation is that you can't emerge like a lottery winner. If you're out $5,000 back pay because your employer or union fired you illegally, you'll probably be entitled to collect only the $5,000 you lost, *not* $5,000 under each separate law!

I do live in one of EEOC's model cities and I've received my notice from EEOC of a fact-finding hearing that I'm to attend. What'll happen at the hearing? Will I need a lawyer?

EEOC's three model offices—and more will likely be added

soon—are trying out new procedures to attempt reconciliation between you and your employer at an earlier-than-usual stage of proceedings, in hopes of diminishing that three-year pile-up EEOC is staggering under. The kickoff procedure is to hold a fact-finding hearing within weeks or months after you file, not years as was the case before.

In theory the hearing is an opportunity for the EEOC investigator to literally find out the facts in the case by gathering information from both you and your employer simultaneously. So, both of you will be required to show up at the hearing. It's not a formal, court type hearing—the investigator takes notes for the purpose of probing the facts later. And you and your employer will be encouraged to make a settlement right then and there.

Is a lawyer needed? Your employer will have one there and your employer's lawyer will subtly try to trap you. He will try to have you answer questions in a way most favorable to your employer and most detrimental to *your* position. That's the lawyer's job! The EEOC investigator may or may not see the trap before determining whether you should answer and you're *not* required to answer questions put to you directly by the employer's attorney. But remember the EEOC investigator isn't there to see that you win your case, only that the case is ultimately resolved. So, having your own attorney—one familiar with EEOC procedure—ensures you representation of your interests. He or she can ask your employer the same kinds of subtle questions, based on a knowledge of applicable law.

The unofficial reason EEOC holds these hearings is to facilitate settlement of your claim and that's another reason for bringing in your lawyer. Your attorney can help you fashion a "settlement remedy," advising you whether a particular job or dollar amount offered by your employer is reasonable in view of your probable chance of success at a *formal* EEOC hearing or a court trial.

If you can't retain counsel, and you live in a city with an active working women's organization—such as Chicago's Women Employed—you can learn what to expect at the hearing from a *non-attorney* advocate.

Suppose I win a sex discrimination lawsuit under Title VII or some of the other laws covering my employment rights. What's the employer's penalty? And what do I get?

It depends—on your case, on the type of discrimination, and on who it affected.

Did it affect just *you*, several women who have the same job as yours, *all* the women at your company, or all the qualified women who've applied to your company, but have been turned away simply because of their sex?

What kind of discrimination? Lower pay? Fewer fringe benefits? Inequality in promotions? In job assignments? Sexual harassment? Tampering with your seniority? Firing pregnant women despite their ability to continue working?

A plus C but not B? All of the above? The more women affected, and the more extensive the type of discrimination, the greater the penalty on the employer.

Some companies have been penalized by court orders that prevent them from engaging in future discrimination at the risk of contempt of court order! Occasionally, the employer losing a sex discrimination case—or, realizing his odds, and settling before trial—is required to take affirmative action in recruiting, hiring, and promoting women.

When the court orders affirmative action, it's to correct the imbalance already caused by the employer's illegal discriminatory practices. And this is one of the *rare* situations in which a private (non-government) employer must engage in affirmative action, despite rumors to the contrary. Specified as a penalty for proven, past illegalities, this kind of corrective affirmative action will probably *not* be viewed by the courts as reverse discrimination.

What are other remedies? EEOC, your state's fair employment practices agency, or the courts may order back pay based on the salary you lost because of your employer's illegal practices, reinstatement to your job if you were illegally fired, a promotion if it was illegally denied you, a transfer, recognition of your seniority, punitive damages, and your attorney's fees. Sometimes, the other costs you incurred in bringing your case—which, above and beyond your attorney's fees, are often in the *thousands* of dollars—may also be awarded you if your case reaches the courts, but this is an exception.

How about big bucks? We've all read cases of women being awarded phenomenal sums, but these are the exceptions that prove the rule. What rule? That you'll have almost no chance of collecting more than you actually lost, without a lot of speculation. As discussed before, don't expect to wind up with a windfall. If you were illegally denied a promotion that carried a $3,000 raise, you may find yourself promoted and you may even get the $3,000. But the court, in any lawsuit, won't award you damages based on your unsubstantiated opinion of what *could* have been. So, bring your lawsuit, but don't make a down payment on that private island!

If I file a charge of sex discrimination against my employer, what's to stop him from firing me for that reason alone?

The law—specifically, our old friend Title VII.

You're entitled to file a *second* charge with EEOC on the basis of retaliation. Title VII specifically prohibits an employer from getting back at an employee who exercised her legal rights by filing a complaint.

What if you're not fired, but life is made miserable for you in other ways? Being badgered, being given a much heavier workload, being put on a shift with less desirable hours—that's all harassment, and it's called retaliation.

How about if your employer retaliates by telling you your work isn't up to par and then fires you on that basis? Again, you're entitled to charge that you were fired because of that first complaint you filed.

Throughout, you've been referring to working women's organizations. What are they and where do I sign up?

They're non-governmental, non-union groups whose function is to help the working woman get a better break. While there are many of these organizations, ten in particular are widely known for getting results. These ten deal primarily with the non-executive group, especially office and factory workers.

How can these groups help? After receiving complaints from women in particular industries—banks and insurance companies are popular targets—or specific companies, they negotiate with management to try to correct discriminatory practices voluntarily.

Why should employers listen? Because among these 10 are some formidable heavies. Women Employed, for example, has wrestled Chicago's Harris Bank to its knees after lobbying in Washington to have the institution's federal deposits withdrawn as a penalty for its sexist employment practices! The case is still pending. But employment lawyers on both sides of the issue stand in awe of this little group's guts and results.

On the home front these organizations serve as an informal clearinghouse for employment gripes. Consequently, they know when one particular company is a big offender, and they've facilitated EEOC's filing of class action suits as a result.

What if you're not in one of their cities? Contact the closest one, and ask whether they know of a similar group in your town. Or contact the National Commission on Working Women, 1211 Connecticut Avenue, N. W., Suite 400, Washington D.C. The phone number is (202) 466-6770. Their list of organizations that can help you is spectacular and current! Here are the ten mentioned above:

Working Women's Organizations

Advocates for Women
  256 Sutter Street
  San Francisco, CA 94108
  415/391-4870

"9 to 5"
  140 Clarendon Street
  Boston, MA 02116
  617/536-6003

Cleveland Women Working
  3201 Euclid Avenue
  Cleveland, OH 44115
  216/432-3675

"60 Words Per Minute"
  PO Box 29091
  Washington, DC 20017

Dayton Women Working
  c/o YWCA
  141 W. 3rd Street
  Dayton, OH 45402
  513/228-8587

Women Employed
  5 S. Wabash
  Chicago, IL 60603
  312/782-3902

Women Office Workers
  680 Lexington Avenue
  New York, NY 10022
  212/688-4160 or 5837

Wider Opportunities for
  Women
  1649 K St., N.W.
  Washington, DC 20006
  202/634-4868

Women Organized for
  Employment
  127 Montgomery St., #304
  San Francisco, CA 94104
  415/566-0849

Working Women Organizing
  Project
  1258 Euclid Ave., Rm. 206
  Cleveland, OH 44115
  216/566-8511

Displaced Homemakers' Entrée to Employment

My mother is fifty-five years old and has spent most of her adult life keeping house for Dad and us kids. Now she's divorced and has no immediately marketable skills. Are there any special laws for women in her situation?

Yes!

Right now, there are over three million displaced homemakers in the country—women over thirty-five who have been divorced or widowed, who have never worked or who may not have worked for years outside the home. Recently progress has been made in helping them achieve economic independence through employment.

Why the need for that kind of help? If life insurance hasn't provided enough, how about alimony, Social Security, or welfare until jobs are found?

In the first place, some of these sources don't even provide enough money to bring a woman up to the poverty level. Only 14 percent of all divorced women receive alimony and their awards average only

$3,000 a year. And, of these women, only half ever actually collect any of those support payments.

True, Social Security widow's benefits have been extended to the *divorced* woman who was married for at least ten years. But unless there's money coming from somewhere else, she'll have to spend her middle age roofless and hungry because she can't collect those benefits until she's sixty! (The exception is if she's caring for her and her former husband's minor child.)

Welfare might be available to many displaced homemakers who can't find work. But special requirements must be met. Rent must not exceed a certain amount, for example. The homemaker who's been left with the home she's been making is generally barred from receiving welfare even if all mortgages are paid off and she has no money to live on while she tries to sell the house. And although she may qualify for government food stamps, welfare is generally not available to the woman who's managed to find part-time work. Besides, who really wants to go on the public dole as a matter of choice?

Help is on the way and some of it's here already. Because more than half of all women over sixty live in poverty in our nation, Congress has recently approved the Displaced Homemaker Assistance Act. Follow-up federal legislation will be on its way to provide funding for the establishment of special centers to help displaced homemakers become economically self-sufficient. These centers will provide job and education counseling, information about available scholarship funds, job and job training referrals, job placement, even referrals to free and low-cost legal, medical, and mental health services.

More than half the states have—or are about to have—legislation setting up displaced homemaker centers of their own. They're already in force in California, Florida, Maryland, Massachusetts, Minnesota, Nebraska, New York, North Carolina, Ohio, Oregon, and Texas. And an Illinois law, introduced by state representative Susan Catania, who chairs the Illinois Commission on the Status of Women, has also earmarked funds for centers aimed at helping displaced homemakers find the kind of work they want and need.

If your state doesn't yet have such a center, you might find that a variety of non-governmental centers in your area provide similar services. To learn more, try contacting your YWCA, other community service organizations, your state representative, or The National Alliance for Displaced Homemakers, 3800 Harrison St., Oakland, CA 94611.

My mother is a displaced homemaker. She says she's unemployable because she has no job history. But she's always been treasurer of ORT, coordinator of community fundraisers, even the head of the PTA. Don't these skills deserve legal recognition?

Yes, and they do receive it! The United States Civil Service Commission now recognizes volunteer experience as being equivalent to paid employment history. Plus, displaced homemaker centers have resources to advise the mature job-seeker about how to translate that experience—how to emphasize and describe various skills she's acquired and used as a volunteer—when she interviews for a paying job.

Nearly half the states have—or soon will have—employment guidelines for state employees to recognize and evaluate volunteer experience.

Some private businesses are formally beginning to recognize the management skills and organizational talent it takes to run a blood drive, a synagogue film festival, or a hospital auxiliary shop; so the dynamo who's done these kinds of things need not check "none" in the employment application space for "work history"!

Sexual Harassment

My boss keeps proposing that I sleep my way to the top. He doesn't mean solitary catnaps at my desk. Is the law becoming more responsive to the problem of sexual harassment at work and at school?

Yes!

Only recently has sexual harassment come out of the closet. And that's because women have typically responded to the situation with shame and embarrassment, as if they had somehow provoked unwelcome advances. Most women never seriously thought they were entitled to be free of such behavior at their work place, and simply endured it until, thanks to a small but persuasive number of women, the law recently began to recognize sexual harassment as a legitimate problem.

What constitutes sexual harassment? Not just physical abuse. Repeated comments, propositions, any form of demeaning, unwelcome advances qualify too. When you've made your position clear and the conduct persists, that's sexual harassment.

Recently, a case was decided in federal court under Title VII of the Civil Rights Act of 1964. The decision: Sexual harassment is indeed a form of unlawful sex discrimination *if* it is a condition of employment. That means that if your employer or supervisor indicates directly or indirectly that your job—or a promotion—depends on your sexual cooperation, if you're actually fired for not cooperating, or if you refuse to be pleasantly receptive to lewd suggestions, you may have grounds for a lawsuit.

If you do, it's not just the boss you're bringing to task, but the company, too, thanks to a new, encouraging precedent set by the federal courts. Previously, the conduct of the individual pest (unless he were the *employer*) was viewed as having nothing to do with the overall company. The corporation had no responsibility to set a standard of discouraging such behavior. Not any more; now the corporation can be responsible for this kind of abuse and can be sued.

You don't have to put up with sexual harassment to get that promotion and you don't have to tolerate it to get an *A* in chemistry either. You may remember the suit brought by several undergraduate women against Yale University, after students allegedly were coerced into having intercourse with at least one of the instructors to be assured of a passing grade. The students' charge: The university "failed to combat sexual harassment of female undergraduates . . . and denies equal opportunity in education."

Yale University denied that it was legally responsible for such complaints. But in preliminary hearings, a magistrate determined that one of the six women plaintiffs indeed had a valid basis for the suit. She was a direct victim, she was still enrolled at Yale, and *she had tried repeatedly to have the university intervene in her behalf*. According to the magistrate: "It is perfectly reasonable to maintain that academic advancement conditioned upon submission to sexual demands constitutes sex discrimination in education, just as questions of job retention or promotion tied to sexual demands . . . have become increasingly recognized as potential violations of Title VII's ban against sex discrimination in employment."

Who was to blame? The university, said the magistrate: "When a complaint of such an incident is made, university inaction then does assume significance, for [in] refusing to investigate, the institution may . . . be held responsible for condoning . . . the discriminatory conduct."

The case hasn't yet gone to trial. But the magistrate's initial determination that the student has a legal basis for a suit—not just against the individual teacher, but against the university itself—is a significant legal coup.

Where should you turn for help? The state division or commission on human rights in your state may have some power to assist victims of sexual harassment. For example, after an employee of Monsanto Textiles charged sexual harassment, the New York State Division of Human Rights assisted her in receiving a settlement of $10,000. Right now, New York is the *only* state that keeps separate and distinct records of all sexual harassment complaints—proof of its expressed, deep commitment to helping victims of this form of sex discrimination.

If you'd like more information about your rights in this area, contact Working Women United Institute, 593 Park Avenue, New York, NY 10021. This group is an excellent source for legal and other referrals, speakers and workshops as well as a legal clearing-house. WWUI has prepared a state-by-state evaluation of progress in laws pertaining to sexual harassment, and a national legal network is the result of those efforts. If you're filing a claim against a school, an employer, or the unemployment insurance division of your state—on the basis of sexual harassment or refusal to be granted unemployment benefits because you were fired or you quit as a result of sexual harassment—turn to WWUI. You or your lawyer can receive copies of all briefs (lawyers' arguments filed with the courts) where the facts of the situation match yours. It'll be a great savings of both time and money for you and your attorney.

If I quit my job because of sexual harassment, can I collect unemployment benefits while I look for other work?

Maybe!

Historically, the unofficial stance of the claims processor was often, "Can't you take a little teasing?" Consequently, a sexually harassed woman would often list a personality clash as her reason for leaving. That just doesn't qualify for good cause. If we're all adults, we should all be expected to tolerate some degree of conflict in our lives.

But now that women are recognizing—and acting on—their right to be free of such abuse, the issue is being presented *directly* more and more to unemployment insurance departments across the country. Although such legislation is pending in New York, Wisconsin, and elsewhere, *no* state *yet* has a law that explicitly says that sexual harassment is good cause for leaving. But, at the same time, no state has a law that says that sexual harassment is *not* good cause for leaving. What all of this boils down to is a lot of leeway for deputies and adjudicators, the people who initially process your unemployment insurance claim.

Many claims adjudicators make factual determinations about sexual harassment much the same as they would about any other cause. They might ask if the incident occurred between the worker and her boss, in which case the problem would be extremely difficult to resolve, or was it a colleague, even a subordinate, doing the harassing? In the latter case intervention from personnel might have been effective. Did the woman report the incident? Was the offending incident repeated after a warning? Was the contact verbal or physical? Repeated or an isolated instance? If an isolated but very disturbing incident, did the victim quit within a reasonable time afterward?

She who hesitates may be losing her claim to benefits. Here's one situation that proves the point. A woman alleged her boss had tried to force her to have sex with him, although he ultimately desisted. But she didn't quit her job until three months after the incident occurred, during which time he made no further advances. Her dilemma is easy to identify with: Most of us try to stick things out and make the best of a bad situation, but the rage and anxiety eventually make it impossible for us to do so.

When the claim for benefits came up, the adjudicator found the sexual harassment to be reasonable grounds for leaving but, because of the time delay, the adjudicator determined that harassment may not have been the *real* reason she quit. The woman didn't appeal the decision; of course, the adjudicator's judgment is not a statement of law.

Occasionally, a woman will make a discreet report of sexual harassment to the personnel department and then find herself abruptly and mysteriously fired. If that happens to you, you have the right to claim that sexual harassment precipitated your dismisal.

Right now, almost every state has litigation pending on behalf of women whose claims for unemployment insurance were flatly and specifically denied on the basis that sexual harassment is not sufficient cause for leaving employment. What will come of it all? Lawyers working in the area of unemployment insurance compensation predict that sexual harassment *will* soon be generally acknowledged as a basis for voluntary leaving with good reason.

And with good cause. New case law precedents that apply to analogous situations are pointing the way. New decisions, for example, say that unemployment insurance benefits can be obtained for psychological reasons, i.e., intense stress, caused by specific factors involved with a particular job. More important, sexual harassment, like rape, is less often misunderstood for something it's not. Changing attitudes finally recognize that the woman isn't "asking for it," and the public is finally aware of the seriousness of the problem. Those realizations are putting pressure on the law.

Unemployment Compensation

What qualifications are there for drawing unemployment insurance benefits?

Assuming your work is insured work, and most work is, despite myths to the contrary, you must establish two things: good cause for leaving your job and "ability and availability" for employment!

But it can be tricky because "cause" and "ability and availability" are the two most widely litigated areas in the field of unemployment insurance law.

For financial reasons, an employer very often challenges the "good cause" given by an employee who quits. If the employer is reluctant to pay out additional funds in benefits, he may try to establish that the employee's reason for leaving was not what the law considers to be "good cause." (Some of the reasons a woman will consider as good cause, but the employer, department of unemployment insurance, or the courts will *not*, will be explored in the next few questions.)

An employer will often step in when an employee has been fired under certain circumstances too. For example, an employee who has been discharged for "willful and wanton conduct" probably cannot collect benefits or, in some states, will have to wait six to eight weeks to do so. Her claim for benefits may be challenged by her employer, but she'll have an opportunity for a hearing to present her side of the story.

The employee who is laid off because her employer has a lack of work runs the least chance of her claim to benefits being challenged on the basis of cause.

But once the "cause" roadblock has been cleared, the "ability and availability" hurdle must be vaulted before benefits can be collected. Sometimes "cause" can be combined with "ability and availability" as the reason for denial of benefits. An example? If an employee quits to stay home with her children, in some states, she has flunked both tests.

If I quit without good cause, can I be denied benefits?

Maybe!

If good cause to leave can't be established, the unemployment insurance laws of more than half the states *absolutely* prohibit an employee who quits her job from collecting benefits.

Other states allow an employee to collect benefits even if her reason for leaving doesn't meet the good cause requirement. But these states subject her to a penalty waiting period before she can collect those benefits.

In Illinois for example an employee who quits without good cause can't begin to receive her benefits until six weeks after the "wrongful leaving." But, once the benefits begin, she's entitled to receive them for the *entire* twenty-six-week benefit period, just as she would if she had quit with good cause or had been laid off.

There is one common denominator in every state: A woman is entitled to unemployment insurance benefits only for the time she is actually "able and available." So, if your former employer can show that you're not looking for work, your benefits stop. And, of course, once you've found new work, you're not officially looking and the unemployment insurance checks must stop coming.

If my boss fires me, am I guaranteed benefits? I'm "able and available" for work.

No!

This is an unfortunate misconception about the way the unemployment insurance system works. Some employees want to quit and believe—incorrectly—that they can collect unemployment insurance benefits *only* if they're fired. So, they'll deliberately throw in a monkeywrench to bring down the axe. But if the employer can establish that you were warned about your errors and deliberately persisted anyway, you may very well find your right to benefits being challenged by your former boss. (Not to mention your bridges being burned for a good job reference.)

But, in general, unless your behavior was truly outrageous—to the point of deliberately screwing your company—it's very difficult for an employer who fired you to challenge your right to collect benefits. Remember though that an employer may *always* challenge on the basis that you're not legitimately seeking employment.

I'm pregnant and was laid off work. I'm still capable of working, though, and I'm looking for a job now. May I collect unemployment insurance?

Yes!

For that bundle of joyful news, you can thank the Supreme Court for delivering an opinion in a landmark case. A law that *presumes* that all pregnant women and new mothers are unable to work is unconstitutional, the Court said.

Here's what happened. In 1975, Utah was one of nineteen states whose unemployment insurance laws had special disqualifications for claims from pregnant women who quit or were fired for reasons having nothing to do with their pregnancy. Utah's law specifically and automatically made pregnant women ineligible for unemployment insurance benefits for a total of eighteen weeks—twelve weeks before, and six after, the blessed event.

A case against the state was brought by Mary Ann Turner, who had been laid off work for reasons unrelated to her imminent motherhood. She received unemployment benefits and looked for a full-time job. But then, even though she hadn't found work, the benefits suddenly stopped appearing—exactly twelve weeks before her due date. It wasn't quite what Turner was expecting! And, when she inquired, Utah's unemployment insurance bureau explained how the state law prohibited a pregnant woman from receiving benefits for that eighteen-week period. Meanwhile, although Turner wasn't able to find a full-time job, she *did* work as a temporary clerical employee.

Turner had been turned down for benefits during an eighteen-week period when the Utah law *presumed* she was not "able and available" for work, but she had in fact held down her temporary clerk spot during that very same time. And those were circumstances the Supreme Court pointed out in reaching its decision, explaining, "It cannot be doubted that a substantial number of women are fully capable of working well into their last trimester of pregnancy and of resuming employment shortly after childbirth."

The Utah law was declared unconstitutional. "Freedom of personal choice in matters of marriage and family life is one of the liberties protected by the Fourteenth Amendment," the Supreme Court said. And it emphasized that the Constitution requires a more individualized approach to determining whether a worker's pregnancy actually interferes with her "ability and availability" for the labor market.

The decision in this case does *not* require benefits to be paid to a pregnant woman who is incapacitated and unable to perform full-time work. But it *does* bar the state from *presuming* that a woman's pregnancy automatically takes away her "ability and availability" status.

I'm pregnant, and my obstetrician suggests I leave my job. On her advice, I'm voluntarily quitting. Would any state allow unemployment insurance benefits under these circumstances?

Maybe!

What is it about your job that your obstetrician feels is harmful for you at this time? Lifting heavy weights? Breathing noxious fumes? Being on your feet all day?

If a *change* of employment is necessary but you're still available for *full-time* employment in the same or a similar field, you may be successful in collecting benefits while you're looking for suitable work. Although many states are liberalizing their stand on the situation, nevertheless, it still depends on the state you live in.

Technically, you're not required to limit yourself to the same or a related field for a new job. Logical career changes are generally recognized as valid reasons to look for greener pastures. What's logical? Quitting your job as a garage mechanic to look for work as an auto-parts sales clerk, especially if you've had some recent experience along those lines, would probably be considered good cause. If you quit your job as a garage mechanic to look for work as an astrophysicist, good cause would be a little tougher to prove.

The state's main concern, however, is that a pregnant woman may not be truly able and available for employment. So your efforts in looking for work in a similar industry will be more persuasive. This is especially the case if you indicate to the person handling your claim that you're available for a variety of different positions and have some decent, recent employment experience to back you up.

While you're pounding the pavement, it's crucial to document your job search after voluntarily quitting. Write down the names of every company you call for interviews, the dates you made contact, the names of all the people with whom you spoke—even if you didn't get an interview. If your claim for benefits is denied, you may appeal. But, as in all situations involving unemployment insurance, you *must* be able and available. That goes even for the period when you're not receiving benefits because you're waiting for the appeal or waiting for a decision on the appeal. And any time you're not able and available—even for a week—you'll be denied benefits for that time.

In any event, it's clear that you may *not* be denied unemployment insurance benefits on the sole basis that you're pregnant.

I work in a store where I have no ready access to a phone. I want to quit this job and look for a desk job where my children can call me when they get home from school and touch base with me once or twice a day. Do any states consider this "good cause" for quitting?

Probably. The law is changing in your favor!

At one time, more than twenty states had *specific* regulations interpreting family obligations or marital obligations as insufficient cause for leaving a job.

But now, thanks at least in part to changing attitudes toward the acceptability—and necessity—of mothers working, most states are looking more kindly on the situation. Family reasons are more and more frequently regarded as good cause for quitting in the majority of states and benefits are allowed.

The question "Why didn't you think of that in the first place?" is likely to pop up. But there are factors that persuade the state in your favor. The length of time you held the job makes a difference, and the longer, the better. You may have had a change in the family situation. For example, for the past year, you had good help, but now you don't. The ages of your children are taken into consideration—if they're junior high age or younger, your request would be considered far more reasonable. And a change in the job structure—if you had access to a phone when you took the job, but you lost access when the store was reorganized—will count too.

What will you need to do? First, you must establish that you made a reasonable effort to explain your situation to your employer and to work out an arrangement that satisfied both of you. If, for example, your company has a strict policy against calling an employee away from the floor except in an emergency—or of simply discouraging personal calls—did you try to work out a compromise? Did you and your employer consider having you take your breaks to coincide with the time your kids come home from school or other arrangements that would let you get to a phone for ten or fifteen minutes?

If you tried a compromise like that for a reasonable period of time and it didn't work out, did you tell your employer, to see if a different compromise could be reached?

If you show you tried everything possible to accommodate your employer under the circumstances, the unemployment insurance department is likely to react favorably to your request for collecting benefits.

My mother lives with us and used to take care of my children all day while I worked. Now she's too old, and I can't afford a babysitter. The only solution I can work out is to look for night work to ease the load on Mom. Can I collect unemployment insurance while I look?

It depends on your occupation!

First, as discussed earlier, not every state regards obligations to your children as good cause for leaving a job. But, even if your situation doesn't come under the good cause category, some states will let you collect benefits after a penalty waiting period.

Second, some states may give you a hard time on the able and available issue when you quit to shift from day to night work. The position of these states: You're not really able or qualified to do the work you claim you're available to do. If you're a pediatrician's receptionist, for example, such states might point out that it won't be easy for you to find a new job where you punch in at two in the morning. But, more and more, states are not allowed to *presume* your inability.

When will you have little or no trouble with this roadblock in your situation? When the kind of work you do could be done day *or* night; i.e., nursing, certain kinds of factory work, some kinds of computer work, hotel clerking, and some supermarket jobs.

Can I collect extra unemployment benefits to cover my husband and children?

If you have supported them, yes!

Technically, the amount of benefits you receive is based on your previous earnings, not on current *need*. But, in some states, you're entitled to extra benefits if you have dependents.

It was the unemployment insurance system policy in some states, until recently, to *automatically* award extra benefits to a male claimant who said that he had dependent children. On the other hand, women—especially married women—who claimed dependent children were forced to *document* the fact that they contributed more than half the children's or spouse's support. Thanks to a storm of lawsuits, *all* states have dropped this discriminatory practice. Now states have an option in setting up a uniform policy. They can require *both* male and female claimants seeking dependent benefits to document their claims. Or they can make their award procedure automatic, no matter which sex the parent or spouse is.

My husband just got promoted to Vice-President of the firm. But the firm is transferring him to another state. This is a big break for him, and there are good career opportunities for me in the state we'll be moving to. Could I collect unemployment insurance while looking for work in our new state?

In most states, yes!

About 80 percent of the states specifically regard this kind of marital obligation as good cause for quitting.

It's ironic though that some states' attitudes are paradoxically sexist on the subject. When it comes to unemployment insurance laws, some states won't grant benefits in situations like yours. But when it comes to divorce laws, some of those same states hold that a woman can be regarded as abandoning her spouse because she *didn't* quit her job to follow him!

I was laid off my job. I'm able and available and looking for a full-time job. But I'm going to school during the day, and I was denied unemployment insurance benefits for that reason! Can that be legal?

Yes!

Not all states have laws that say unemployment benefits can be denied to someone attending school in the daytime. But if a state *does* have a law like that, it's within its rights, according to the U.S. Supreme Court.

The case that led to the decision was brought by Marlene G. Smith, who had been laid off her job as a retail clerk. She would have been eligible for unemployment insurance benefits under the laws of her state, Idaho, except that she was a day student, attending classes from 7 a.m. to 9 a.m. She had specifically chosen crack-of-dawn classes so that she could look for work as a salesperson, since most stores in her city didn't require employees to report to work until 9:30 in the morning.

According to Idaho's unemployment insurance laws, night students could collect benefits, but day students could not, because day students aren't able and available for full-time employment. But the Idaho Supreme Court agreed with Smith, who had brought her case all that way herself, without a lawyer.

However, the state of Idaho thought that ruling was rotten potatoes! It appealed to the U.S Supreme Court, arguing that its state supreme court decision was wrong. (At this point in the turmoil, by the way, Smith got a lawyer.)

What happened? Some justices noted that the Idaho Supreme Court would be entitled to regard "night school" as including classes from 5 p.m. to 9 a.m.—before the normal workday starts, and including the hours Smith was working.

But the U.S. Supreme Court decision was in favor of the state of Idaho. "Daytime employment is far more plentiful than night-time work," it said. "In a world of limited resources, a state may legitimately extend unemployment insurance benefits only to those who are willing to maximize their employment potential by not restricting their availability during the day by attending school."

I'm an untenured university professor who has just been given notice. My subject is political science, and the job market just couldn't be worse. What are the chances of my collecting benefits if I stick to my guns and refuse employment outside my field? Outside my city?

It depends!

The more highly skilled the job—and this is especially true of the professions—the more you'll be expected to look for work away from your home city, even your home state, in a tight job market.

If there are only two universities within a hundred-mile radius of your home, you'll probably be denied benefits if you refuse: (1) to move or to commute an incredible distance; (2) to seek employment at one of those two colleges in at least a tangentially related field; or (3) to seek employment teaching political science in a slightly different capacity, e.g., at a high school or a junior college.

You can't be denied benefits, however, for refusing completely unrelated work—slinging hash or chucking trash—at one of the two universities.

But the above guidelines are not hard and fixed. If you've published extensively in one specialty and have made a name for yourself, it would be considered less reasonable to expect you to accept a job in a field only quasi-related to your own. On the other hand, a relative novice in your specialty might be denied benefits for not showing much flexibility.

What can I do if my claim for unemployment compensation benefits was denied because I quit due to sexual harassment, was fired because I reported sexual harassment, was let go just because I'm pregnant, have quit or been fired because of other forms of sex discrimination, or quit because of family obligations that made my job impossible?

Appeal!

If you believe you've been denied benefits unfairly, and you're able and available and looking for work on a full-time basis, you have the right to appeal—no matter why you were turned down.

If your benefits were denied for any of the above reasons, before you appeal you might want to consult with one of the working women's organizations in your city. If your unemployment insurance problem is specifically related in some way to sexual harassment, a good source to contact is Working Women United Institute, 593 Park Avenue, New York, New York 10021, phone: (212) 838-4410. This national research and action center, dedicated to the legal issues of sexual harassment at the work place, can provide you with procedural advice and/or local attorney referrals. And of course if you're out of a job for any of the above reasons, you might consult with a working women's group *before* you file your claim for unemployment insurance benefits too.

Your work situation—the basis on which you were fired or the reason you quit—may *also* be the subject of sex discrimination laws. So you might want to seek your remedies through legal channels available to those who have been discriminated against in employment.

But your immediate purpose is unemployment insurance benefits, so it's important to act quickly. And fast action is essential if you must file an *appeal* because you were denied unemployment insurance benefits. The laws of your state set a time limit for an appeal—sometimes as short a period as a week. So, it's worth the time and money to give a call to the appropriate organization for help in preserving your rights.

What happens at an appeal? You'll be asked to present your case at a hearing, much like a courtroom procedure but not as formal.

You're entitled to have a lawyer (or any other person) represent or assist you, you can have witnesses testify on your behalf, and you can bring in letters, memos, and documents that you feel are relevant. The strict rules of evidence of a courtroom are not adhered to. If you've been denied benefits because your employer protested your claim and the claims adjudicator believed your employer, your employer will be present at the hearing too; and you're allowed to cross-examine him or her. You also might find yourself at a hearing if benefits have been granted to you and your employer has appealed.

Social Security

If I die, can my husband and child receive benefits based on the money I've paid into Social Security over the years?

Yes!

A widower and minor child are now entitled to the same survivor's benefits a widow and her child would receive under the same circumstances.

That's a new change in the law. Until 1974, only women were entitled to draw certain Social Security benefits when they found themselves widowed with minor children. These women-only benefits were commonly called mother's benefits, because they were intended to provide enough support for a woman to stay home and care for the child if the major wage earner died.

But in many families, the major wage earner is the wife rather than the husband. And a legal case that provided a poignant example of the inequities in the Social Security laws led to the Supreme Court declaring this form of discrimination unconstitutional.

Here's what happened in that landmark case. A young couple, Stephen Weisenfeld and Paula Polatschek, were married. Paula had worked as a teacher for five years before marrying Stephen and continued to teach after they became husband and wife. Meanwhile, Stephen had started a free-lance consulting business. Since he earned less than $4,000 a year, the couple lived primarily on Paula's teaching salary. Tragically, two years after their wedding, Paula died in childbirth.

Shortly after Paula died, Stephen applied for Social Security survivor's benefits for his son, Jason Paul, and these benefits were granted. Then he applied for mother's benefits. He received some benefits on behalf of his son, and they added up to less than $250 a month. Why so little? Because, Stephen was told, Congress designed mother's benefits for surviving *mothers* to stay home to rear a half-orphaned child. Stephen also found out that, had he been a woman whose deceased husband had paid into Social Security as Paula had, the mother's benefits would add up to an additional $250 a month which would allow Stephen to remain at home with Jason Paul.

Even if he were working, Stephen would have been entitled to funds through a certain allowance formula if he had been a woman. But as a man Stephen was not entitled to these benefits either.

Stephen decided to fight this discriminatory law. He sued the Social Security agency, arguing that these laws were unconstitutional. Stephen claimed the laws completely disregarded Paula's mandatory Social Security payments, which had been deducted from her paychecks for seven years. And on top of that, he argued, the Social Security laws discriminated against widowed fathers who chose the traditional child-care role.

Stephen's case climbed all the way up to the U.S. Supreme Court—and the Supreme Court agreed that this discrimination was unconstitutional. If a working woman is forced to make substantial contributions to Social Security, should her being a woman prevent her family from receiving benefits from those hard-earned contributions? No, said the Supreme Court. And it acknowledged that, when the Social Security laws were being written in the 1930s, it may have seemed reasonable that a man was financially responsible for his wife and child. But the U.S. Supreme Court recognized that the times have indeed changed. Those archaic generalizations, the Supreme Court said, can't be used to "justify the denigration of the efforts of women who do work, and whose earnings contribute significantly to their families' support." So now mother's benefits are father's benefits too.

But my husband died after we got a divorce. Can I still get mother's benefits to care for my baby?

Maybe!

When your *ex-husband* dies and you are caring for his child (or more aptly your mutual child), the child herself is eligible for certain benefits and *you* may be eligible for benefits too. As long as your ex-husband was your child's father, it doesn't matter who initiated the divorce or that your ex never saw his child after the day your divorce decree was final. And it doesn't matter if you have never worked and, therefore, never paid into Social Security, because these particular payments come out of your ex-husband's Social Security account.

When Stephen Weisenfeld's landmark case was decided by the U.S. Supreme Court, the Social Security laws were changed and your benefits are provided under these new laws. And these laws are *not* discriminatory. For example, if your ex-husband has custody of your child and *you* die, your child *and* ex-husband are entitled to draw the same Social Security benefits.

In either case, benefits are given expressly to allow the remaining parent to stay at home with the half-orphaned child. So if the remaining parent receives some income from employment or freelance work, the mother's benefits are reduced according to a certain formula. But the child's benefits are not affected—she or he is entitled to the full amount. To qualify for the benefits, however, the child generally must be a minor, but disabled adult children also meet the qualifications.

How long must you have been married to your ex-husband for you and your child to be entitled to these benefits? As a general rule, only nine months!

Naturally, the status of your ex-husband's account with Social Security is relevant to such benefits.

Incidentally, a U.S. Supreme Court decision is now pending to

determine whether "mother's benefits" can be paid to a parent who
has *not married* the now-deceased husband (or wife) of the child. An
answer is due in mid-1979.

*I'm divorced, too. But I'm interested in finding out how that status will
affect my old-age benefits. I've never worked outside the home so I have no
Social Security account of my own. Do I have the right to draw old-age
benefits on my ex-husband's Social Security account?*

Perhaps!
Thanks to a very new amendment to the Social Security Act, you
will be able to draw benefits—in recognition of your contribution
as a homemaker to you and your husband's financial well-being
during your marriage. If you had been married for at least ten years
before your divorce and haven't remarried since, you may be
entitled to draw your old-age benefits on your ex-husband's Social
Security account.
Not very long ago, you would have been denied these benefits if
you were divorced before a twenty-year marital stint! But the laws
changed because this twenty-year restriction was especially unfair to
the older, displaced homemaker. Consider, for example, a woman
whose husband divorced her after eighteen or nineteen years of marriage. The entire time she had exclusively performed the traditional
role of the homemaker, had never worked outside the home, and so
had no Social Security account of her own. Also she didn't receive
alimony. By denying her old-age benefits on her ex-husband's account, the Social Security laws were denying her financial recognition of her input into the family's livelihood.
The genuine contribution of a homemaker not only to the
couple's financial well-being but also to her husband's ability to be
the outside breadwinner is finally recognized in the new amendment. Theoretically, there's no way an ex-husband can prevent his
ex-wife from collecting by showing that she wasn't a good homemaker or that he wanted her to get a job outside the home.
Right now, the amendment doesn't extend quite the same rights
to an ex-husband whose ex-wife was the only one who brought a

paycheck home. Although the circumstances are the same, he is not entitled to draw benefits on his ex-wife's Social Security account. Since this restriction doesn't give "equal recognition" to the Social Security payments the ex-wife was forced to contribute, it's very likely that this form of discrimination will be struck off the books soon.

What happens if both partners are wage earners? My husband and I both work, but I've always earned more money than he has. When we retire, will he have the right to collect old-age benefits on my Social Security payments over the years?

Yes.

Under the present rules he'll have the option of drawing benefits on the account which is higher—yours or his. In addition if you die, your widower is entitled to draw extra benefits based on your account when he reaches sixty years of age. In this regard, he has the same rights to special benefits that a widow would have.

Until recently, the law assumed that the husband was the primary breadwinner. A widower was forced to prove that more than half his support was provided by his wife, something a widow never had to do. Now, *both* widows and widowers are required to indicate to the Social Security Administration that they're claiming benefits on the account of the spouse who provided more than half the family income. This is called "proving dependency," but it is not as onerous a procedure as the poorly phrased term implies.

Despite non-discriminatory changes in the law, one inequity remains. As long as a woman is not married when she seeks her widow's Social Security benefits, she is entitled to draw on her deceased spouse's account. For example, Martha was thirty-five when her husband died. Martha remarried, but she later divorced her second husband. When Martha turned sixty, she was eligible to draw on her first husband's account.

Martha enjoys these rights because she is a widow, but a widower in identical circumstances does not. Once he has remarried, despite the fact that he's sixty and single again, his deceased wife's account is closed to him. Again, the courts are slowly but surely striking down such discriminatory laws, and this one may well be struck down soon.

Pensions

Frankly, I haven't paid much attention to my company pension plan. Retirement is forty years away! Besides, I draw a pretty good paycheck. Why should I be bothered by a pension plan?

A good pension plan is money in the bank for your twilight years. Thanks to advances in science and medicine, we're in an age when women can expect to live past seventy. But at present statistics show that the average woman past sixty-five is literally destitute. A good pension plan is a good hedge against becoming part of those statistics.

More than thirty million workers—more and more of them women—are covered by private pension plans. Plans usually fall into one of two categories: contributory, in which the employee pays into the retirement fund, and non-contributory, in which the employer foots the bill.

In either case, an employer-administered pension plan is part of your total compensation package. So why doesn't your employer just give you a bigger paycheck and leave the saving and investing to you? Primarily because the employer gains tax advantages in paying you with a pension plan. But also because the small amount withheld from your paycheck is pooled with sums from all contributing employees to enable greater investment potential for your dollars.

But remember, with a pension plan as with everything else, there's no such thing as a free lunch. Your pension plan, like your salary, is not a gesture of corporate affection or generosity. It's part of your pay for work you're doing *now*—although you'll benefit from it in the years you may need those dollars the most.

Employed women are beginning to recognize what men have known for some time, that fringe benefits, including pension plans, are a valuable part of an employee's compensation. So it's important to pay close attention to profit sharing, stock options, and retirement benefits your company may offer, and to view those perks the way your employer views them: As compensation for work done in lieu of a higher immediate salary and with certain tax advantages to both parties.

Certainly you wouldn't turn down an exciting job in your field with great growth potential but no retirement benefits to accept a stagnant position that couples mind-crushing tedium with a dynamite pension plan. But know your options!

I'm paid the same salary as the three men in our firm who do the same work I do. These men have been given the option of including their spouses in the company pension plan, but I haven't been given this choice. My company says the option is limited to employees who are the principal wage earners of their families, and my husband earns more than I do. Are there laws that give companies the right to do this?

No!

In fact, there are laws against it. Under Title VII of the Civil Rights Act, an employer may not discriminate between men and women with respect to retirement benefits, including pension plans. Benefits and options based on head of household or principal wage earner requirements in pension plans offered by employers are therefore generally unlawful too. And paying you fewer benefits than a male worker receives for the same job is as unfair as paying you less cash—and just as unlawful under Title VII.

Can my employer require me to pay more for my retirement benefits than a man with the same job would pay? My company argues that I'm not being denied benefits by this system, nor are options being offered to men that aren't available to me. But my employer points to those statistics that show women live longer than men and consequently he says we should be required to pay more for benefits, because we'll collect benefits for a longer period after retirement. Has anybody ever challenged this line of reasoning?

Yes. And when the women working for the Los Angeles Department of Water were given this argument, they took their case all the way to the U.S. Supreme Court where the Department was held to be all wet.

The Department's theory was that unless women as a class were assessed an extra charge they would be subsidized to some extent by male employees. But the Supreme Court noted that the pension plan provided for survivor's benefits. If a worker dies, his or her spouse receives the benefits. And, looking at those longevity statistics, the court turned the actuarial tables on the Department: If women are said to live longer than men, then the *female* spouses of male employees would probably have a greater life expectancy than the *male* spouses of female employees. So subsidies paid by male employees for coverage of female employees would be more than made up for since those employees' long-lived widows would be eating up the Department's pension plan dollars. When it came down to it, the whole subsidy system was unfair to everyone.

But the heart of the Supreme Court decision lay elsewhere. The court reasoned that longevity statistics may have some basis in fact, but only as a sweeping generalization. Each individual woman forced to pay more for her pension benefits couldn't be relied on to die according to an actuarial schedule.

So, some individual women, fated to die earlier than some individual men, would be shortchanged by having had to pay more for their benefits than any man had to pay.

The dissenting Supreme Court Justices argued that statistical prediction is at the heart of all group programs. But the majority of the Court looked to the wording of Title VII, which makes it unlawful for an employer to discriminate against any individual with respect to his compensation because of such individual's race, color, religion, sex, or national origin. So the court held that Title VII's use of the term "individual" precluded an employer from using even a true generalization—in this case, actuarial statistics—to discriminate against an entire group protected by the law.

Because a court rules on the facts of the case it's hearing—a pension plan, in this instance—the Supreme Court did not extend its ruling into analogous areas, health and life insurance plans, for example, administered by the employer. And, since the court's decision was based on Title VII, it dealt only with pension plans that are part of employment benefits—so the subject of privately purchased pension plans, not administered by an employer or a union, was not addressed. But with this case as a precedent, it's likely that similar lawsuits will be brought by both female and male workers required to pay different amounts for insurance benefits.

My company pension plan must have been excerpted from Through the Looking Glass! *How can I tell if I'm being treated fairly when there's a semicolon after every other word? Must I hire a lawyer to help me wade through this document?*

No!

Because of the diverse quality of pension plans—and evidence that millions of employees were not receiving what they thought they were entitled to—Congress passed the protective Employee Retirement Income Security Act of 1974 (ERISA).

For the working woman who's concerned with her total compensation package, ERISA helps in two very important ways. First, the law sets minimum standards for employee pension plans. And second, ERISA requires your employer to provide you with an *easy-to-comprehend summary* of your rights and obligations under the company pension plan.

You're also entitled to written disclosures that explain the financial well-being of your pension plan as well as regular statements showing the amount of accumulated benefits owed to you.

If I quit my job or am fired, do I lose the money I've paid into my pension plan?

No, thanks to ERISA!

If you've been with the company five years—or less, under some plans—you have the right to your pension plan contributions as well as the earnings they've made. But you'll probably be an older woman before you see the money.

ERISA now prevents the employer (or union, if it's a union pension plan) from keeping your contributions when you change jobs.

ERISA also prevents an employer from keeping all the money it paid in on your behalf as compensation to you for your work.

You certainly don't expect to stay with the same company from your first day out of school until your retirement party and no company expects you to! Retirement benefits aren't the reward for forty years' service. That's why the gold watch was invented. Retirement benefits are a deferred payment to you for work you do *now*.

At some point, the money you pay in for your benefits, the money contributed on your behalf by your employer or union, and the amount that contributed sum earns becomes *yours*. You have a vested right or vested interest in that money!

Now, when do you collect? According to ERISA, you have a right to all your contributions, some of the employer-paid contributions, and certain benefits after five years of service. But, if you're a young person, you'll collect only 25 percent of your contributions when you leave, and the company can take fifteen years to dole out the rest. No matter how old you are, you have a right to *all* your benefits after ten years of service. But, if you leave on your tenth anniversary, you'll collect only 50 percent with the rest payable to you for each of the next five years.

Those are ERISA's minimum requirements. Your individual company plan may well be more liberal about when you have acquired a vested interest in the benefits and about when you can run to your mailbox for the money. Be sure to read the summary of your own pension plan.

I've heard people refer to the "housewife pension plan." What's that?

That's IRA for spouses!

The tax-sheltered Individual Retirement Account was created for people who are not eligible for a union or employer-sponsored pension plan. If your spouse meets that essential requirement, then you qualify for a spousal IRA. And, although spousal IRA is sometimes nicknamed the "housewife pension plan," it's equally available to men who are full-time homemakers.

Here's how it works. The worker who qualifies for IRA can set aside up to 15 percent of his or her earnings to a maximum of

$1,500 per year in the tax-sheltered plan. But, if the worker's spouse—typically, a homemaker—earns no money, the couple can now start a spousal IRA. Now, the worker can contribute up to $1,750 a year for both husband and wife. But equal contributions *must* be made for both spouses; for example, if a couple sets aside the maximum amount, $875 must be put into the husband's account and $875 must be put into the wife's account. If the couple is divorced, each still owns his or her account independently.

The special tax advantage is that your IRA contributions are deductible from your gross income at tax time. And the money in your IRA earns interest, but unlike a regular savings account the interest is *not* taxed each year. Instead, the interest is taxed when you draw your benefits, generally at age sixty-five. You'll very likely be in a lower tax bracket at that time than you are during your current and middle-age peak earning years, so the tax you'll pay then will likely be much lower than the tax you'd pay on interest in a savings account now. So you get a double tax benefit, the deduction when you set the money aside, and the deferral of taxes on the interest until your taxes go down.

You can start withdrawing your benefits as early as age fifty-nine and one-half. And you may take out money before that, but you'll pay tax penalties if you do.

If you're in your twenties, contribute the full $1,750 for the next forty years, and get the highest interest rate available, you'll have an incredible retirement nestegg of over $400,000. But will that amount seem so mind-boggling when you actually retire? Maybe, but just in case, experts agree that the maximum $1,750 limit will be pushed up in the years ahead to keep pace with inflation, no matter how sky-high it goes.

And, by the way, cohabiting and lesbian couples are discriminated against under IRA. It's a married-only program.

I'm getting divorced. My husband doesn't make much money and claims he has no assets, but he has a fairly good pension plan with his company. Does a property settlement ever include a percentage of pension rights?

It might!

This situation isn't cut-and-dried in *any* state. But your chance of being entitled to this asset in a community property state, California, Idaho, and Louisiana, for example, has improved since a recent California court decision. According to that decision, certain rights to participate in pension programs are actually community property rights. So that means that your husband's rights in his pension plan could be divided the same as any other community property. But even in a community property state not all types of pension plans fit neatly into the court's ruling on that decision. And in non-community property states the rules are even less clear-cut.

For the older, divorcing woman—who may not have marketable skills and who may face age-discrimination in the job market—rights to her spouse's pension can be crucial. Be sure the divorce lawyer you select is familiar with this fast-changing area of the law. Because, depending on the type of pension plan and your state's laws, you may receive payments from your ex-husband's plan when he retires, or immediately in cash.

Taxes

Is it my imagination, or am I suffering a tax disadvantage for being a working wife?

You're suffering, and you're not alone.

Recently, a working married couple filed a lawsuit against the Internal Revenue Service to demand a refund of $1,220—the amount they alleged they were forced to pay because they were living in rather than out of wedlock. But Judge Philip Nichols Jr. of the U.S. Court of Claims found their position taxing. He refused to strike down the discriminatory provisions of the IRS laws, stating that, "Tax disparities will exist no matter how the rates are structured. This is simply the nature of the beast." Instead, he advised men and women to consider cohabitation, suggesting that opposition to such arrangements by law and custom has for all practical purposes been eliminated in our enlightened society. (Keep in mind, though, that his statement is not necessarily legally accurate—and is *not* legally binding.) "Couples can now," explained the judge, "enjoy the blessings of love while minimizing their forced contributions to the federal budget."

Nevertheless, working wives who prefer a legally blessed lifestyle still resent the unholy tax burden. So, alone and through various organizations serving the employed woman, they've been lobbying Congress for an amendment to IRS laws that would give married couples in a two-worker household the same tax status that cohabiting couples enjoy.

If the IRS laws smile benignly on one change in lifestyle, they don't on another. In the 1940s, 80 percent of all U.S. households were composed of working husbands and non-working wives, the basis on which the laws were formulated. But now that arrangement occurs in only one-third of our country's households.

What causes the tax trouble? "Aggregated income" and "graduated taxes"! The graduated income tax forces the two-earner family, filing jointly, to be viewed in aggregate by IRS, as if it were, according to its 1940s conception, *one* wealthy man! And filing separately still generally doesn't put the married worker in as advantageous a position as her single sister with the same salary.

Especially unfair, feminist economists and accountants agree, is the burden on the married family in which the wife is the "secondary" earner. She's not working to build a career, in other words, but to supplement her husband's income. But her "secondary" earner position ends up putting a primary burden on the family's taxes. If she earns even four or five thousand dollars a year, and her husband earns ten thousand, her addition to the family pot can cause the family tax bracket to skyrocket.

I'm pregnant, and I wonder whether I'm entitled to special tax deductions, either now or when the baby is delivered.

Yes and no!

As with the treatment of any other medical condition, the cost of your care—including the cost of *traveling* back and forth to the doctor and the hospital—is deductible. And medical supplies—the post-episiotomy sit-on ring, for example—plus lab tests and x-rays are deductible, too. If your doctor recommends you wear special support elastic stockings, you might be able to run these up as a tax write-off as well. But non-therapeutic maternity clothes, from nursing bras to hatching jackets, are *not* deductible.

Diaper services, alas, are not deductible, nor is the salary of a practical nurse or other aide that cares for the baby unless the baby, as opposed to mom or dad, is ill. If your doctor insists on a particular infant formula for a medical condition your baby has, or a vaporizer or air filter for her room, check with your accountant. Items like these, which you might buy to have on hand just in case, probably are not tax deductible for a healthy baby. But you might be able to deduct them if the doctor prescribes them as part of a sick baby's treatment.

I'm a working mother, and I pay for childcare. Do I get a tax break?

Yes!

IRS provides for a direct childcare credit of up to $400 against your income tax if you have one child under 15, up to $800 if you've got more than one. Under the new law, you qualify for the credit whether the babysitter comes to your home or you send your child to nursery school, day care, even camp!

If your main babysitter is your mother or another relative, you're entitled to the tax credit based on what you paid her. That's provided she's not your dependent, and her income is subject to Social Security taxes. Check with your accountant to see whether you'd be better off with or without the credit in this situation.

If you're divorced, working, and have child custody, you may be entitled to the credit, even though your ex contributes more than half the child support, and even through your ex, not you, is entitled to claim the child as a dependent on his IRS return!

My husband and I are divorcing, and we're trying to work out an equitable property settlement. Are there certain tax advantages and disadvantages that go along with dividing up certain kinds of property?

Yes!

Tax-wise, it can be just as costly to give away some types of property as it is to accept others! Have your accountant—or a tax lawyer, working in consultation with your divorce lawyer—review a list of all your assets, including real estate, stocks and bonds, insurance and pension policies. They'll be able to suggest lawful ways you, your children, and your ex-husband can wind up with more and the IRS with less!

If you happen to take stock, for example, consider what the tax consequences might be for your ex. If your husband gives you stock that's gone up in value since it was purchased, he'll have to pay a capital gains tax on that increased value, even though he hasn't sold the stock! (Naturally, the same would be true if you gave him your stock.) On the other hand, some properties may result in taxable income to the spouse on the receiving end.

And the IRS views a lump-sum settlement made to the wife and children (or husband and children) differently from the way it views staggered payment of alimony and child support.

Some tax consequences surrounding divorce may of course be inevitable. But it makes good sense to avoid all the extra taxes the law permits. Make sure your lawyer is familiar with all the ways 'tis better to give than receive, and vice versa!

3

In the Marketplace

Insurance

I'm interested in purchasing life insurance. Will I have a hard time? Are there special problems facing women who buy life insurance policies?

Yes!

Recently, the states of Pennsylvania, New York, Colorado, Michigan, and Iowa undertook significant studies of sex discrimination practices in granting life insurance. These studies—which have been given great credibility by legislative bodies in many states—unearthed a number of sex discriminatory practices that some insurance companies are guilty of.

There are various life insurance options available to men that are *not* generally available to women. Men, for example, are frequently offered the opportunity of increasing their insurance coverage at the time of key events, i.e., marriage or the birth of a child, *without* having to have a physical examination or otherwise present updated evidence of good health. This is *not* always the case for women. In addition, women don't always receive the favored rates in such situations that men would be entitled to.

Women's rights seem to be waived when it comes to the waiver of premium option, too. This option allows the life insurance policy to continue without further premium payments in case the insured becomes totally disabled. This option may generally be purchased by men in *all* risk classifications, but is restricted only to women in *low*-risk classifications. Some companies offer policies that require women who seek the waiver of premium option to prove that they're employed outside the home. But men are *presumed* to be so employed, and are neither questioned nor denied coverage on this point.

A married woman's insurability and rates are assessed, by some insurance companies, on the basis of her *husband's* credentials. According to a report prepared by the Women's Equity Action League (WEAL), "Insurance companies commonly limit the amount of coverage available to a married woman not to exceed the amount of coverage held by her husband. The reverse is rarely true, even when a woman is the principal wage earner in her family."

The effect of such practices? The woman who out-earns her husband and is in better health may be sold only the more expensive, high-risk insurance because her husband, if he had applied for the policy, would be considered a high risk! This practice is apparently never reversed. A wife's high-risk status is not relevant to the policy purchased by her husband.

WEAL and other sources also report that mothers of illegitimate children are often denied life insurance policies. But the legitimacy of a man's children is not as often specifically questioned when the man seeks a policy.

What can you do? If you find you're being denied insurance coverage, or you're offered a policy with sex discriminatory features such as the ones described, notify the insurance commissioner of your state. The commissioner will usually but not always be located in your state capital. He will be listed as Director of Insurance, Superintendent of Insurance, Commissioner of Insurance, or Insurance Commissioner of your state. In addition, you might want to contact Women's Equity Action League, 733 Fifteenth St. N.W., Suite 200, Washington, D.C. 20005, for more information and current referrals to other helpful sources.

Some states, including California, Michigan, New Jersey, North Carolina, New York, Pennsylvania, Colorado, Arkansas, Idaho, Iowa, Nevada, Ohio, Tennessee, Wisconsin, and Texas, *do* have specific regulations prohibiting sex discrimination in insurance. Industry practices in those states are said to be improving. If discriminatory insurance policies are offered through your employer, remember that you may have a cause for action under Title VII of the Civil Rights Act of 1964—the federal law that prohibits sex and pregnancy discrimination in employment fringe benefits, *including* insurance coverage!

In any event, shop around before you buy. Since more and more women are demanding better service, some insurance companies have realized the business advantage in abandoning sex discrimination practices.

How about homeowner's or renter's insurance and automobile insurance? Is there discrimination there too?

Yes!

Women often experience difficulty, according to WEAL, in getting property and liability insurance, especially because of their marital status—no matter what it might be!

Those state-sponsored reports found that married women have a tough time getting property and liability insurance in their own names because insurance companies *prefer* to write the policies in their husbands' names.

Women aren't exactly allowed to go in high gear when they apply for car coverage either. Women whose husbands don't drive are often questioned by their insurance companies about why the husband won't be included as a driver on the wife's policy. But that isn't true in reverse. A simple statement like "My wife doesn't drive," apparently puts the brakes on questioning when a man applies for a policy.

Single and divorced women have been denied property insurance coverage for their homes, "presumably because they're apt to leave their homes for longer time periods than married couples, widows, or unmarried men," according to WEAL.

And there are also reports that newly divorced women are forced to re-apply for auto insurance if their prior policy was in their spouse's name. Women in this situation are treated by their own insurance companies as brand-new customers and may be forced to pay higher premiums, because divorce places the policyholder in a higher risk category.

The divorcing man, on the other hand, seldom faces this road-block. He simply drops his ex-wife from his existing policy. And even if both paid the premiums, the policy remains in the husband's name. (Naturally, you're not required to set up your insurance application in this manner, but it's still a prevalent custom.)

And WEAL reports that the state study found, in the manual of one insurance company, a warning to agents to be cautious in writing policies for women who don't have custody of their children after a divorce. But similar restrictions, applying to men who don't have custody, were non-existent.

All these problems are being attacked by the legislation of many states. Your state may already have legislation prohibiting this sort of conduct. To find out, check with your state insurance commission.

I'm pregnant and expect to work until I have the baby. If I should experience complications, though, does my employer have the right to exclude me from the company's disability insurance policy?

No! New legislation has passed amending Title VII of the Civil Rights Act to specifically prohibit discrimination on the basis of pregnancy, childbirth, or related conditions.

Why was the legislation necessary? The legislation was introduced right after a 1977 landmark decision by the U.S. Supreme Court, which had ruled that *no* existing law prevented an employer from discriminating against pregnant workers in its disability insurance policies. The U.S. Supreme Court hadn't been convinced that Title VII of the Civil Rights Act, as it was then worded, required pregnancy-related disabilities to be covered just as other disabilities would be.

The case was brought as a class action by women who worked for the General Electric Company. The women explained that they were not requesting disability insurance for all pregnant workers at GE—just for those few whose doctors had determined that actual, but temporary, disability existed. The GE policy had specifically excluded any insurance coverage for disabilities related in any way to pregnancy.

Pregnancy is *voluntary*, argued supporters of the insurance discrimination. If there are complications resulting in some kind of disability, it was because of the woman's own choice. So she alone should pay for the consequences, not her insurance policy!

But, argued the GE women, look at the procedures for which GE *was* perfectly willing to extend disability insurance coverage: injuries resulting from participation in sports, disability arising from elective cosmetic surgery, temporary disability arising from the circumcision of a GE worker—even hair transplant complications! The women pointed out that they were all voluntary medical procedures, or disabilities resulting from participation in a voluntary activity, like football, and all entitled a GE worker to draw disability insurance benefits!

How then, argued the GE women, could this *not* be evidence of unlawful discrimination? And the Supreme Court had an answer. GE management, the high court concluded, had simply viewed all of its employees in one of two categories: Either pregnant persons, or non-pregnant persons. Ruled the extreme arbiter of justice, the court of last resort: GE is not discriminating against its *women* employees; it's merely discriminating against *"pregnant persons."* Because some *non-pregnant* persons are *women*, the court concluded, no discrimination existed! (You remember how that goes: All dogs are animals, all animals have four legs, therefore all four-legged animals are dogs.)

And the U.S. Supreme Court itself partly retreated from its own position just a year later. This time it held that a pregnant worker who had taken a mandatory leave of absence due to her pregnancy could not lose her seniority upon her return to work.

Now that the new pregnancy legislation clarifying Title VII is in force, the U.S. Supreme Court's decision on General Electric is no longer law. Why? Because the decision was based on the fact that the court thought Title VII did not technically bar this type of insurance discrimination.

Credit

In general, what does the new Equal Credit Opportunity Act (ECOA) do for working women, married or single?

Plenty!

That new federal law gives women the right to have credit in their own names—*without* regard to their husband's income or credit history. It gives the woman with an income of her own the right to be deemed credit worthy based on *her* earnings, *her* history of paying off bills, and certain other factors that a creditor uses to predict whether you'll be a good credit risk. In other words, for the first time, it gives women the non-discriminatory right to credit where credit is due.

How does a creditor determine, under ECOA, what kind of risk you are? First, he can't have one set of standards for men, another for women. For example, if a creditor wouldn't ask a man certain questions such as, "Do you plan to have children before your condo is paid off?" he's not allowed to ask that question of you. And, in the past, even though a man and a woman earned equal salaries, women were more frequently required to have a co-signer for a loan or credit card. But now, if a creditor wouldn't require certain things—like a co-signer—of a man, he can't require them of a woman either.

In general, a creditor may evaluate the *type* of job you have in determining how good a risk you'll be. But if your creditor would extend credit to a man with the same job, income, and bill-payment history as yours, he can't deny extending credit to you. Excuses like, "Well, you're a *woman* selling insurance, and people will be less likely to buy insurance from a woman, so your income might not be as stable," is the kind of thing ECOA just won't buy either.

Problems can still come up because creditors are allowed to closely scrutinize the income of people working part-time or free-lance, before granting them credit. This practice is not literally a form of sex discrimination, but it particularly affects women because women do make up most of the part-time work force. And more and more, women are engaged in some kind of free-lance work or self-employment on a non-professional and/or small-income scale.

Another extremely significant plus under ECOA is that marital status *cannot* be a factor in a creditor's decision to make a loan or issue a credit card or charge account. The creditor cannot require a single woman to show extra credit-worthiness just because she's single or divorced. A creditor cannot view a married person as a better risk or more stable than a divorced or single person. And a married woman's income cannot be disregarded or discounted when she—or when the married couple—apply for a loan or credit cards. Formerly, mortgage lenders would discount the working wife's income assuming that she would probably quit work to have children because, they reasoned, why *else* would the couple be buying a three-bedroom house in the suburbs?

There is an exception to ECOA because of some state laws. In community property states only, a woman will still be required to obtain her husband's signature for credit cards or loans just because those community property laws give her husband an automatic interest in her earnings. Under those laws, her income isn't entirely hers to spend, so she alone can't promise Visa that her every cent will be available to pay back all her debts. But it works both ways. The husband in a community property state will also have to have his wife's signature on his credit application for the same reason. However, even in these states, if a woman is relying, for credit, on money not subject to community property laws—inheritance money for example—her husband's signature can't be required.

What else does ECOA do for you? One of its most important features gives you the right to a credit history in your own name. This right is available for the first time to both working and non-working married women. As of June 1, 1977, if both husband and wife are authorized to use a new account, the account must be reported in both spouses' names. If you hold credit accounts established before that date, you're entitled to notify the creditor that you want credit information to be reported in your name as well as your husband's. This way, you'll both have history to your credit.

Does ECOA do anything else for the non-working married woman?

Again, plenty!

If both husband and wife have been responsible for an account, those credit-history reporting provisions of the new act permit a full-time homemaker to have the payment history recorded in his *and* her names. This does *not* mean that a woman with no income of her own can easily get credit in her own name, although she may have a joint account with her husband. It *does* mean that, when and if she has an income of her own and wants credit in her own name, she'll have a credit history of bill payment. That credit history—coupled with her income—will be evaluated by the creditor in determining whether she's entitled to credit in her name alone.

This way, if you're widowed or divorced and go to work, you'll be able to get the credit you may need right away, based on the history of bill payment you established with your husband. And, if you remain married but go back to work, you'll be able to get credit in your own name then too. One result of the new law is that you and your husband will be able to obtain *more* credit than you could before ECOA, assuming the credit history was a good one!

Do you mean that before ECOA a married woman had no way to prove to a creditor that she had ever paid a bill in her life?

Yes!

Before ECOA, when an account or loan was in the husband's name, creditors didn't have to report the track record of borrowers, credit card holders, and charge customers in the wife's name and most did not! Consequently, most credit bureaus had no history that a married woman existed, much less paid off bills!

Failure of equal credit reporting had devastating effects on most married women, both those who worked outside the home, and those who exclusively shared their husband's paychecks. A married woman with no income of her own, for example, may have handled all the household finances, budgeted for all the family's needs, paid all the bills with her own or a joint checking account, and, in general, made sure each bill was paid on time. The charge plates she used may even have had her name on them and she may have co-signed their mortgage loan. But meanwhile, her twenty or forty years of sound money management were legally being attributed to her husband only because the accounts and loans were in his name. As long as the couple stayed married, no real problems were likely to come up. But upon divorce, or the death of the husband, the woman found she had not an iota of legal proof that she'd ever been responsible for paying a dime.

The newly divorced or widowed woman, settling into a new job and applying for a charge account or an auto loan would be told that no record existed of her ability to pay bills. And, in a small town, creditors who got wind of the change in her marital status could legally close down all the couple's existing charge accounts—even call in outstanding mortgage and auto loans before they were due!

The woman who'd worked throughout her marriage, or for part of her married years, wasn't spared a whit of this discrimination either. A woman who contributed to the family income—or who actually supported a husband and children—was still a non-person to her creditors, although they lost no time suing her—and her husband
—when she defaulted.

Before ECOA, married women who insisted on credit cards and loans in their own names may have had their good credit record reported in their names. But before ECOA, a woman was seldom issued credit in her own name! Why? Because there was no federal legislation to convince her creditors that the color of her money wasn't any different from her husband's.

I don't make much money, but my husband works too, and, between us, we make a good living. Do I still have the right to apply for credit based on his salary?

Yes!

You have the right to advise your creditor of every source of income available to you. When should you exercise this option? Only when your own income is too low for credit to be granted to you.

The extent of credit you want will make a big difference. If you earn about $12,000 a year, for example, your income alone may be high enough to get you credit in some places on your own without regard to any other sources of income you might have. Your local pharmacy, say, may let you charge a few hundred dollars worth of drugs and disposable diapers, based just on your own income, the fact that you live in the neighborhood, and are a frequent customer. In this case, the charge account should be in your name. If your income and credit history are adequate, it's unlawful for a creditor to refuse you credit in your own name.

But suppose you want an American Express or Diner's Club card, permitting you to charge virtually any amount. (Generally, these types of charge cards have no ceiling, but all charges must be repaid with thirty days—no mounting interest!) These creditors demand that an income higher than $12,000 be available to pay what you charged on that madcap, whirlwind escape to the Canary Islands.

In these cases, you have a choice—forego the card, or show your creditor that you do have more than your $12,000 salary as available income. If you choose to rely on your husband's income in this situation, the creditor has the right to investigate his credit history. And it's most likely that the credit will be issued jointly, i.e., in his name with you as merely an authorized user.

To ensure that you develop your own credit history, insist that the account is listed in both names—*not* Mr. and Mrs. George Washington, but Mr. George Washington and Mrs. *Martha* Washington. If your card arrives as Mrs. *George* Washington, protect your right to a credit history. Send the card back and request that a new one be issued in the name of Mrs. Martha Washington.

My husband doesn't exactly have a reputation for wise money management. Does ECOA require his credit history to be linked with mine?

No!

Under ECOA, you're entitled to be considered for credit in your own name, regardless of marital status, based only on your income, your job, your credit history, and other non-sexist factors reflecting your credit-worthiness. If you take advantage of this right to separate credit accounts, you generally need not provide any information about your husband. (The only exceptions are in community property states, discussed previously.)

If you do go it alone, that means you cannot permit your husband to use your account. If you let him have this responsibility, the creditor is entitled to know about his credit history, and credit information on the account will be reported in your husband's name as well as yours!

If you want to keep a clean slate—if you want your record to be free of references to your spouse's poor credit history—your spouse must not apply for joint credit invoking your good name and income! Otherwise, you'd be making credit history together, in both names.

If I do exercise my option to have the creditor take my husband's salary into account, can the credit card still be issued in my own name?

Maybe!

Once you trigger things by asking the creditor to consider your husband's income in determining your credit-worthiness, you don't have quite the same right to credit in your own name. You'll at least get a joint account, linking you with your husband. But the fact that the bills were paid (or not paid) will be reported in your name as well as your spouse's.

If you meet certain qualifications, or come close—i.e., your income is only a bit below the creditor's bottom line, you have a stable low-risk profession, live in a "good" neighborhood, and own property in your own name—it may still be possible for the credit to be issued to you exclusively rather than to both of you jointly. (However, a complex system of "credit scoring," only now beginning to receive investigative attention, may link credit-worthiness to other, non-income factors.)

A history of successful handling of accounts in your own name rather than jointly is persuasive to a creditor when you're seeking more credit. Therefore, it's important to have accounts in your own name whenever you can. How does that fit in with ECOA's mandate that you can't be denied credit on the basis of marital status? A joint account suggests that you're married, so why should you be penalized for having one? As the law currently stands, this contradictory issue isn't fully explored, and you're better off for credit purposes to show an independent ability to manage your debts.

Can I be refused credit because my income is from alimony, or because I plan to use child support payments toward the bills?

No!

When you apply for credit, you must be informed by your creditor, according to federal law, that you do not have to reveal the fact that any of your income is provided by child support, alimony, or separate maintenance payments. You can choose to reveal these sources only if you want the creditor to consider them as part of your total financial resources.

It won't be to your advantage to reveal those sources unless your own credit-worthiness isn't sufficient for you to be granted credit on the basis of your earnings and credit history alone.

Again, if the amount of your alimony or other sources of income available to pay bills is too low—or the payments are too infrequently made—to warrant the credit you want, the creditor has the right to turn down your application. But whether your income comes from your job or his cannot be a factor in the creditor's decision to give you that charge plate or loan.

There's a chance the domino theory will go into effect too. Once you voluntarily divulge information about your ex-husband so that the creditor can take a look at his alimony or child support payments to you, you open the Pandora's box of questions about his credit-worthiness. Plus, the creditor is entitled to know whether those payments are actually being made, and statistically it has been proven that most ex-husbands do not live up to their decrees. The creditor, therefore, can request a copy of the written agreement or court order requiring those payments to be made. And the creditor also has a right to investigate how long they've been made, how regularly, and all that sort of thing.

How can you satisfy a creditor in this situation? Keep records— including photocopies—of the checks he sends you. What if you suspect, when you're being divorced, that you won't immediately be able to rely completely on your own income to convince a creditor that you'll be able to make the payments? Have your lawyer help you prepare a signed statement from your soon-to-be-ex granting your creditors the right to check his credit bureau files. (Your lawyer might prefer that this be written into the divorce settlement.) This won't make your ex-husband liable for any debts you incur; so don't run up bills thinking that such a statement makes your ex-husband responsible for paying debts you won't be able to! The agreement is merely a way to ensure that support payments he's obligated to make to you and the kids can be taken into account when your creditor is deciding whether to consider those payments as your resources.

Won't my divorce lawyer suggest this? Not necessarily. ECOA is still a very new law, and not all lawyers are familiar with its provisions concerning alimony and child support payments. So you bring it up!

I work part-time during the hours my kids are in school. Can a creditor disregard my income because it's not from full-time work?

No!

But the creditor is entitled to consider the probable continuity of your income. He's not allowed to predict whether you'll continue working at the job, but he is allowed to consider whether the job itself will continue to be available to you.

If, for example, you have a summer job with a roller coaster or a hot dog stand, in a northern city where your job just doesn't exist during the winter, you may have trouble getting credit, whether you work there full or part-time. On the other hand, some high-paying seasonal work, for example construction work, is regarded as having a probability of continuity by some creditors. And school teachers aren't denied credit even though they're not in their classrooms all summer long. So don't assume you can't get credit. If you've been turned down on this basis, make sure the creditor knows that you do this work every year and that you have other sources of income, or other persuasive factors. (And, if you're still denied credit, apply someplace else. Creditors have different bottom line requirements.)

If your part-time work is regular—you work every morning or several full days a week—the income you earn can't be disregarded just because it's generated from a few rather than forty hours a week.

But, of course, you won't be guaranteed credit. If the bucks you bring home don't add up to what the creditor considers enough, and if you don't indicate other sources of income, you can legitimately be refused that charge card because you just don't make enough money.

Can a creditor require me to have my husband co-sign for a loan?

Only in community property states, or if you're pledging his boat as collateral! While a creditor can't require your spouse to sign on the dotted line too, there are occasions when a creditor will request a co-signer for his own safety. A co-signer is someone who accepts the responsibility to make payments if you default. So, if your own income or credit history can't get you a loan, you may be asked to produce a co-signer.

But who you produce is entirely your choice. If the co-signer is credit-worthy, the bank cannot legally object on the basis that your co-signer is not your husband. (One exception: In community property states, each spouse has a legal claim to the other's salary. So the bank may require your husband's signature, unless you can show that you could satisfy the debt from assets belonging to you alone, assets not subject to the community property laws. The other exception is, if you're securing the loan with collateral partly owned by him.)

Before ECOA, it was typical for banks to ask a woman to produce a male co-signer, especially if she were seeking a car or business loan. The federal law won't tolerate this monkey business any more and prohibits lenders from making that discriminatory request. Asking for a co-signer of a specific sex is now legally analogous to asking for a co-signer of a specific race. ECOA makes both illegal.

When is the bank forbidden to request a woman to produce a co-signer? When they wouldn't make the same request of a man with your income, credit history, and other qualifications.

My husband and I use different surnames. Can a creditor require my account to be issued in my husband's surname?

Absolutely not!

The law provides that you're entitled to apply for and obtain credit in your own name. If your own name isn't the same as your husband's, that's nobody's business, including the creditor's. Here, it makes no difference whether you're applying for your own account or for a joint account with your spouse.

Recently, a Lake Forest, Illinois, grocer was successfully sued for denying a married woman credit solely on the basis that her surname was different from her husband's. "Any time you want to reapply under your married name," the grocer insisted, "I'll open the account!"

The woman changed neither her application nor her attitude, and her attitude cost the grocer a $2,000 award to the woman. He's also under court order to change his credit policy.

Along the same lines, if your credit application asks only whether you're Dr., Mr., Mrs. or Miss, you have every legal right to ignore these choices, indicating *no* "courtesy title" or writing in "Ms." yourself, since it wasn't courteously provided in the first place.

How should I proceed if I think I'm being denied credit on the basis of sex or marital status?

Very carefully!

As a practical matter, a good first step is to advise the store's credit manager or the bank's top officials, that you believe your application for credit has been denied on a basis prohibited under federal law. If you do this in writing, it's wise to keep a copy of your letter, then send the letter by registered, certified mail, with return receipt requested. Often, the policy of a store, bank, or car dealership *will* be to abide by federal laws, but the individual employee who handled your request may not understand the new requirements. If that's the case, just sending your letter will usually get results.

If you're not satisfied with the credit manager's response, you're entitled to write to the governmental agencies in charge of enforcing ECOA with regard to the kind of credit you're seeking. When you write to those agencies, send a copy of your letters to the organization that denied you credit. Again, keep copies of all your correspondence, and send your letters by certified or registered mail, keeping the receipts.

Who do you send those letters to? It depends on the kind of credit you were denied. If you've been denied credit by a state bank, your State Banking Association may help you. The credit application you filled out (and which was denied) should have provided you with the name and address of the federal agency having jurisdiction over the particular creditor and he's *required* to give you that information. If he does not, you can write to the Bureau of Consumer Protection, Federal Trade Commission, Washington, D.C. 20560. Or, if it was a federal bank that denied you credit, you can write to the Office of Saver and Consumer Affairs, Federal Reserve Board, Washington, D.C. 20551. If these agencies don't happen to be the ones directly responsible for enforcing ECOA with regard to your particular credit denial, they'll help you find the agency you're looking for.

And, if you prefer, you can have your attorney handle the whole matter for you. But be sure to give him/her copies of all the correspondence you've engaged in. The law does not require you to contact either the creditor who unlawfully denied you or the enforcing governmental agencies before you file suit against that creditor. So, you may want to discuss the pros and cons of your options with an attorney.

4

Crimes against Women

Battered Women

I know that wife abuse has been going on for a long time. Why haven't the police or the courts done much about it?

Historically, the same legal doctrine that terminated a woman's rights at the time of her marriage specifically conferred upon her husband the legal right to inflict mild physical punishment on his wife. Although this right has long since been abolished, its echo remains in our culture.

At least one reason the problem continues is because of women's own history of silence on the subject. Many victims of wife-beating have been ashamed to seek legal help or even to tell friends and family about their situation. Some are afraid of scandal, of having their "usually stable" husbands viewed as sick, or of being thought of as "sick" themselves. Some fear they'll be viewed as low-class, despite statistics that show this crime knows no income boundaries. And some simply blame themselves for the situation.

Economics is another hurdle, since the husband often controls the family finances. If a woman wants to leave, and she has children, is neither employed nor employable, she may have little practical chance of escaping her situation. She may be entitled to public aid for herself and her children, but she may know of no place to take refuge until she can apply for welfare. And, under these circumstances, she's seldom likely to have her husband arrested or to retain counsel and sue him.

Where else must the blame for failing to offer protection for victims lie? With the police and judges, primarily male, who represent the cultural standards of society. In any other context, the police and the courts recognize that assault and battery are criminal actions that give rise to civil liability as well. But, when it's between family members, well, it's "none of the state's business."

And, finally, many women avoid taking action for fear of aggravating an already bad situation. That is, many victims fail to press charges, fearing the reprisals of their husbands or boyfriends. Others drop the charges after the arrest has been made, out of fear, guilt, and occasionally because of their treatment at the hands of the law enforcement system. Other women are discouraged from pressing charges by the police who tell them to "kiss and make up."

Well, I'm not one of those women who won't speak up. I've decided to take legal action against my husband. How can I find a lawyer who'll help me? What if I have no money of my own?

It's essential to find a lawyer who understands your situation. Unfortunately, many lawyers still share, with some police and judges, the same misconceptions about battered women—that you may have been "asking for it," that a man is entitled to hit his wife once in a while, and on and on. Many private lawyers are hesitant to work with clients who are battered women, and you don't want to choose a lawyer who's skeptical about either your reports of the situation or the seriousness of the offenses.

Can you find free or low-cost representation? Maybe. Legal aid organizations and legal assistance agencies are generally sympathetic to battered women's issues and their services are available to lower-income clients. But these agencies are frequently bound by tax-related rules that require the family income to be below a certain point before you can be helped. Your income, in other words, may be determined by what your husband earns as well as by what you earn. If you earn nothing, but your husband earns a good living, you still may be disqualified for low-cost legal aid! These rules, though, may be changing in the near future. Also, different legal aid groups set different income limits. So do investigate these resources!

The Center for Battered Women in Chicago, for example, is one of the first legal assistance organizations to work with battered women who have no money of their own, no matter how high their husbands' income may be. Plus, some law schools have clinics where your husband's income may not disqualify you from free or cheap legal aid.

If you are over the income limit for legal aid, these same legal assistance organizations can often provide you with referrals to private attorneys sympathetic to problems like yours, some of whom may handle your case on a sliding scale fee basis. Who else might be able to refer you to an understanding lawyer? Try your local women's organizations, the American Civil Liberties Union, and your local bar association.

Can the judge require your husband to pay for your lawyer in a battered woman case? Yes, he/she can issue such an order, but be aware that it's often very difficult to enforce.

I want to leave my abusive husband, but I don't have any money, not even enough to get medical treatment for the things he's done to me. I certainly couldn't afford to pay for some place to go to. And, anyway, I'm afraid he'll find out where I go and keep threatening me. Are there any other laws to help?

Yes!

A primary reason women stay in the physical-victim situation is that they have no place to run. Consequently, the new legislation that provides funding for shelters for women as well as their children in this situation is an important counterpart to stepped-up enforcement of criminal penalties. Alaska, for example, has already legislated funding for these shelters, California has crisis centers, and many other states are following suit. Right now, the YWCA, the Salvation Army, and other groups offer free shelter, but these charitable groups have limited financial resources and more state-funded shelters are urgently needed.

The qualifications, as was explained for public aid, are calculated on the family income, the earnings of both husband and wife. But the present public aid laws of most states provide for emergency assistance funds for the jobless, fundless woman, and her children. If they've had to leave because of the husband's brutality, they probably qualify for those emergency dollars and the family income consideration isn't taken into account.

But the "intake" personnel at public aid offices don't *always* know—or respect the fact—that you may be entitled to financial assistance even though your husband is gainfully employed. If the intake person tells you your husband's income disqualifies you for funds, public aid lawyers suggest you insist on filling out a form anyway. If you're formally denied, you have the right to appeal.

You may be entitled to free emergency room treatment too. In addition, in some states, legislation is pending that would allow for the hospital that treats you to be reimbursed through funds specifically set aside for assisting the battered woman.

And don't overlook the obvious! If you have left your abuser, and he's phoning you with threats or harassing you in other ways over the phone, contact the security division of the telephone company. It's against both federal law and the laws of many states to use the telephone to harass and threaten a person! The phone company can direct you to the proper authorities.

If you choose to change to an unlisted number because of harassing calls, tell the telephone company why you're doing it. Sometimes the service charge for converting will be waived if your purpose is to avoid repeated phone harassment.

If the police and the courts won't take my legitimate complaint seriously, is there any precedent for suing them?

Yes!

In 1975, feminist attorney Laurie Woods of MYF legal services in New York found that many of her clients, who had been beaten by their husbands, had been refused police assistance. Even with her legal representation, Woods found, the police and courts were failing to enforce the applicable laws of assault and battery. To help prevent battered women from being batted around by the legal system, Woods flagged the need for a class action suit to compel enforcement of existing laws.

In 1976, the class action suit was brought against the New York Police Department and the family court system of New York, on behalf of battered women who had been refused help by the police or whose assault and battery complaints hadn't been acted upon by the courts.

The suit was successful. In 1978, battered women obtained a decree requiring the police to enforce the laws. The family court issue, however, is still on appeal.

The decree provided that the New York Police Department establish guidelines for handling domestic disputes. And those guidelines made it clear that when a crime is committed by a spouse against his or her mate in front of a police officer—or the officer has probable cause to believe such a crime has been committed—the officer must make an arrest. In determining whether an arrest is appropriate, the officer is not entitled to excuse the violent party on the basis that the couple is married. The officer is legally bound to make the arrest, even though the aggrieved spouse—generally the battered wife—hasn't previously sought a peace bond or has been unsuccessful in getting one in the past.

At the same time, the officer can't refuse to make an arrest simply because the wife has filed a separate legal proceeding against her husband, compelling him to stop beating her.

And the battered spouse cannot be denied the opportunity to press charges simply because the police officer believes the couple can be calmed down or reconciled.

If the crime involved is very serious—a felony, rather than a criminal misdemeanor—the police officer has even less discretion about excusing the violent party. The police officer is not entitled to try to reconcile the couple. The arrest must be made and the violent party removed to police headquarters.

The decree also requires that the victim of any family offense must be advised by the police officer that (1) she may bring a proceeding in either family court *or* criminal court, and (2) the referral of a case to family court, where counseling services are available, is for the purpose of attempting to keep the family unit intact.

Because of the successful New York action, many police departments and family court judges are now more aware of—and more sensitive to—the problems faced by battered women. How about other cities? As a direct result of the New York decree, Chicago's Center for Battered Women successfully negotiated similar guidelines with the Chicago Police Department in 1978 and class action suits like the one in New York are pending in Cleveland, Ohio, and Oakland, California.

Another plus: There's also federal legislation pending that would authorize funds to educate police about the nature and handling of the crime. In addition to helping reduce injury to police who intervene in a domestic fight, it would greatly assist the victimized woman in learning about her rights to file a criminal complaint against her husband. Some states have allocated funds for this purpose already. And federal and state funds for counseling in a family violence situation are becoming available too.

I want to get a peace bond to prevent my husband from physically abusing me. But I've heard that I have to file for divorce first. Is that true?

No!

A judge may be more willing to issue an order prohibiting your husband from entering your mutual home if he/she knows a divorce action is pending. And, in Illinois, and other states with similar new legislation, your lawyer might ask the judge for such an order when your divorce action is filed, or while the action is pending.

But you don't have to file for a divorce in order to be safe from abuse. You have the right to request an order from the judge to enjoin your spouse from threatening you with violence, from beating you, and from harassing you. And, in the same way, an unmarried woman cohabiting with a man who abuses her is entitled to request the court for a restraining order.

In that New York class action lawsuit, it was discovered that police misinformed women—telling them that no arrests could be made unless a divorce action was pending, or without a peace bond. That's not the case.

I've decided to take action against my husband's brutality. What legal proceedings can I bring against him?

Both criminal and civil proceedings are possible!

You're entitled to have him arrested, generally for assault and battery. This requires calling or going to the police. But, to better substantiate your charges, it's preferable for you to call the police to the scene to witness your husband's volatile condition.

Be forewarned: Women's organizations and attorneys familiar with the wife-brutalizing syndrome explain that the police, because of male chauvinism and/or lack of education about the nature of the crime, often try to dissuade a woman from filing a criminal charge. How? By misinforming her about her rights, for example, telling her that it's not a criminal offense if a husband hits a wife, or that it's not a criminal offense unless he threatens her with a weapon. So, know your rights, which are to have the police officer help you make out a criminal complaint against your husband if he has physically abused you.

To help the battered woman file both criminal and civil actions, every state has introduced—and many have already passed—new legislation. An example: In Minnesota, if a police officer is called into a domestic dispute and if he has "probable cause" to believe that the violence complained of has taken place, pending legislation would require the officer to remove the abusive husband or boyfriend from the home and put him in immediate custody.

Other states have proposed that spouse beating be made a felony. It would become a crime, in many situations, carrying a steeper penalty than non-spousal assault and battery. And some states have specifically proposed that the higher penalty also apply to men who beat the women they live with out of wedlock; other states, New York for one, extend specific extra protection to abused spouses.

Also available to you are civil actions. In this area also, new legislation—some passed, some pending—in many states will make it easier for you to get a restraining order. Sometimes called injunctions or peace bonds, they're court documents barring your spouse or boyfriend from bothering you—even from coming near your home. The man who disobeys such a court order is subject to serious penalties for contempt of court.

It's also possible for you to sue your boyfriend or husband for damages—monetary compensation for beating you. Your lawyer can advise you on how your state laws and your circumstances combine for chances of success.

In states that still grant divorce on a fault basis, your spouse's physical cruelty to you will be sufficient grounds almost everywhere. In Illinois, though, the law requires your divorce complaint to allege that the violence occurred more than once. Feminist attorneys view this as analogous to the law concerning legal liability for owning a dangerous canine. Some states say that "the first bite is free," because, only after you've seen the animal bite once can you know you've got a potential killer. But, even under the "one-bite rule," your lawyer can probably sink his/her teeth into a divorce based on grounds of mental cruelty for you.

Rape and Sexual Assaults

If I am raped, what should I do in order to stand the best chance of having my attacker arrested and convicted?

As soon as you realize you have no chance of escaping, start taking a good look at your attacker and remember him. Memorize any scars or markings, the color of his eyes, missing teeth, pierced ears, height, weight, the shape of his face, the color and type of his clothing—every detail that could possibly help you identify him later. Naturally, this will hardly be easy to do under the circumstances, the circumstances being that you're in mortal terror of losing your life. But a good memory now will be your best weapon later. Remembering everything is the one, affirmative thing you can do in a situation in which another has taken control. Let nothing go unnoticed. Even the sound of the attacker's voice, his accent, or pronunciation of certain words can be significant.

At the same time, you can't be too obvious in your mental note-taking. Your attacker is anxious for you not to be able to identify him. If he sees that you're too ambitious along those lines, he may want to make sure you never identify him—or anything else—ever again.

As soon as possible, call the police. Try to get to a place of safety to make your call, but do it immediately. The sooner you call, the better the chance that your attacker may still be apprehended.

Equally important, you should go immediately to the emergency room of any hospital. If you go to the hospital first, have someone there call the police for you right away, although it is better to have the police take you there. Thanks to the efforts of women's groups, many, many hospitals—particularly urban hospitals—now know how to deal sympathetically with a rape or sexual attack victim, and how to collect and preserve the evidence which will help to identify and convict the attacker.

It is crucial that you go to the hospital as is. Do *not* wash your genitals or change your underpants or slacks, no matter how repulsive it may seem not to. If you do, you'll be destroying essential evidence. Your attacker's semen and even pubic hairs can help convict him. If he has injured your genitals and you are bleeding, don't bathe or wipe the area.

Also, make sure that a kindly but uninformed nurse, aide, or doctor at the hospital does not suggest that you go wash up before you are convinced that the proper specimens have been taken. If it does not appear to you that this has been done, wait for the police to arrive and ask the officer to request that proper evidence be taken. Be reassured—the police do not witness such medical exams.

If your city has a rape hot-line or another community service hot-line, call the number from the hospital; they'll probably be able to send someone to you to lend support. If you are in shock and don't have the psychic resources to call the police, the hospital, or a community service hot-line, at least call a friend or relative. If you do nothing, or delay out of fear or hysteria, the odds of your attacker being located, arrested, and convicted dwindle.

Some states still require corroboration of a rape. This doesn't mean you need an eyewitness to the attack, but it does mean that you must have made an immediate report of the attack—if only to a friend or family member—at the time you were still virtually in shock from the incident. Other states accept corroboration within a "reasonable" time after the attack took place. But the longer you wait, the more time you give your attacker to evade the law.

Rape statistics that show up on police records represent only a small percentage of rapes that actually occur, because women still hesitate to report this crime. Women often fear that they will be harassed by the police and the criminal justice system, and, in the past, their fears were not unfounded. For years, rape victims suffered as much or more at the hands of these institutions as they did at the hands of their attackers.

But a variety of organizations have worked hard to change both attitudes and laws and a system is gradually evolving that protects the victim from harassment while preserving the defendant's right to a fair trial. More and more, the police and hospital personnel are becoming educated about what must be done—to gather evidence and to treat the victim with the sensitivity the situation calls for.

If you don't believe the times are changing, remember Wisconsin Judge Archie Simonson, who was promptly voted out of office because of his remarks. After a high school girl was held down by one boy and raped by another, Judge Simonson declared that it happened because the girl was "asking for it" and proceeded to deliver a tirade in general about the dress of modern women. The rape victim had been wearing, at the time, jeans, a turtleneck sweater, and a bulky cardigan sweater over that.

While much progress is still needed in sensitizing the system toward the rape victim, much has been made. Your chances of being made to suffer for having reported a rape are by no means what they once were.

Several years ago, a friend of mine was raped. When her case went to trial, she found it completely humiliating and embarrassing because they dredged up every fact about all the sexual relations she'd had her entire life. Must this happen?

No! Now the federal government and half the states have passed legislation limiting the kind of questions that can be asked of the rape victim.

Previously—and under the laws of some states today—a woman's prior sexual history was considered relevant to the issue of whether a woman consented to the attack. The double standard— "If she let one man do it, she probably let the defendant do it, too"—made a rape trial living hell for the victim.

Some states still allow the defendant's lawyer to tell the jury that a charge of rape is easy to make but difficult to prove. The implication, of course, is that the victim can't be trusted to tell the truth. Called "Lord Hale's" instruction—which gives you some idea of its antiquity—the tactic has been specifically banned in Minnesota, Michigan, and other states.

All of this can be especially jarring to the victim when she discovers that the judge and jury are usually not entitled to be told that the defendant in question has been convicted of rape before. Many a woman finds it unjust that her history is going to be brought up, but that his is not—especially if his history is one of convicted rape. But, with certain exceptions, it's a prerequisite for a fair trial under *any* criminal law that any prior convictions are considered to have no bearing on the defendant and the crime he is currently being charged with. So, in general, they may not be brought up.

Despite theoretical, possible harassment of a victim, in practice the rape trial is becoming another matter. Our lifestyles have changed, and the courts recognize it. Judges are increasingly less shocked by the victim's behavior if an attacker offers as his defense the fact that the unmarried adult woman he's charged with raping lives with a man out of wedlock or otherwise engages in sex. Even hardened defense lawyers have toned down their tactics under the pressure of public opinion, an opinion that recognizes a woman's right to have sex and that views as unfair the manipulation of that right to discredit her testimony at trial. Many defense lawyers now believe that antagonizing the victim by this type of questioning also antagonizes the jury which, naturally, they do not want to do. So your chances of being subjected to this kind of humiliation are not at all what they were even a few short years ago.

Several states—including Colorado, Illinois, Michigan, Oregon, New Hampshire, and Minnesota—have very strong prohibitions against considering any evidence of the victim's prior sex history. Some of the other reform states do permit the defendant's lawyer to cross-examine the victim about her past sexual practices. But, if it is a jury trial, the judge must rule whether the questions the defense counsel wants to ask are indeed relevant and he or she must rule out of the hearing of the jury. In some states, the victim may have her own lawyer, in addition to the state's attorney, present to argue that the proposed questioning is not relevant.

What kinds of questions are—and aren't—permitted? Some states only exclude questioning as to whether the victim has engaged in a certain form of sexual activity. Other states permit questioning about whether the victim has had sex within the past year, if she is single, or if she has had sex with men other than her husband if she is married.

Moreover, there is now a brand-new federal law prohibiting inquiry into the victim's prior sexual conduct. When is this federal "Rape Victims Privacy Act" applicable? When the rapist is charged with a federal offense.

If the woman has ever voluntarily had sex with the man she charges with rape, this fact may be explored by the defendant's lawyer, even in states where the woman's sexual history isn't generally viewed as relevant and even in "federal crime" rapes.

Do I have to use force to defend myself from a sexual attack in order for the attacker to be convicted?

It depends!

The laws of most states, and the case precedents which help the judge interpret the law, recognize that women who are raped may be in genuine fear of losing their lives or of suffering grievous bodily injury in addition to the rape and that putting up a good fight just might provoke a more vicious attack. In addition, it would obviously be unreasonable for the court to insist that you tried to knock the assailant unconscious with a stiff uppercut if he was bigger and heavier than you. The law doesn't require you to hold a black belt in the martial arts in order to convict a man who has attacked you.

Although the criminal justice system is far from perfect in its treatment of the rape victim, things are steadily improving and this is one area in which state's attorneys agree the victim is being treated more fairly.

When the police officer to whom you make your complaint asks you whether you resisted, do emphasize that you struggled and that you verbally resisted your attacker. Also emphasize that, in view of the disparity between your size and the attacker's, you resisted as much as you could, even though resistance seemed futile. Naturally, if you were forced with a weapon, or if your attacker threatened you in any way, make sure you tell this to the police in complete detail. Even the minority of states that do require you to resist to the utmost of your ability temper that strict command with a view to all the circumstances. For example, was your attacker armed or did he appear to be armed? Was he larger than you? Did he threaten greater force when you resisted?

Accordingly, there are fewer horror stories of the rape victim who is cross-examined. Common once but uncommon now is this typical line of questioning:

"Isn't it true, Ms. Victim, that you gave your consent to have intercourse and, only afterward, regretted your cheap behavior?"

"No!"

"Well, did you try to stop him?"

"He had a knife at my throat!"

"Well, did you try to stop him? Ms. Victim, answer my question!"

It's important to explain your resistance in detail when you report the crime. If you have emphasized to the police and, later, to the state's or district attorney, the amount of force you actually used—or the reasons you feared serious injury and did not use force—it's extremely unlikely that your lack of a Herculean counterattack will result in your attacker's freedom. However, you may expect to be questioned about your reasons for not using force.

What if I'm prepared for a counterattack? What do the laws say about the victim's use of deadly force against a man who is about to rape her?

Plenty!

The laws of most states provide for some kind of self-defense against grievous bodily injury. In general, one is not permitted to exceed the force you believe is about to be inflicted on you. But if your attacker is armed—or says he is—the degree of force he's using against you may be considered deadly and your right to self-defense may be equal in measure.

May the force be with you, but don't blithely assume you can send your attacker to an early grave without consequence. When the police arrive and see that you have shot and killed a man, and you explain that you did so in self-defense, you can hardly expect them to say, "Fine, you go home and we'll clean up this mess." You may be arrested for murder and ultimately acquitted because you can convince the judge or jury that you acted in self-defense. But all the circumstances that led you to action will be taken into account. If the assailant has broken into your home, if you have never seen him before, and if he is approaching you or a family member with a gun or a knife, your chances of not being arrested or of being acquitted are better than they would be if the assailant was someone you knew or if you took deadly defensive action outside your home.

Despite widespread publicity given Inez Garcia—the rape victim who went back later to kill her assailant—her case has by no means given any woman carte blanche to do the same. If you truly have no choice in a fast-occurring attack but to kill or be killed—or be maimed—at least know that you'll be in for some heavy questioning and perhaps a criminal penalty.

Is it rape if the attacker does not have intercourse with me but forces oral or anal sex?

It depends on your state laws.

Like all crimes, rape is whatever the law of a given state defines it to be; so there are many different versions.

In defining the crime of rape, some states include a variety of acts involving the genitals of the victim or the attacker. For example, being forced to perform fellatio may not be defined by the laws of your state as rape, but it may be classified as "criminal sexual assault in the first degree" or "carnal abuse." Penetration is explicitly required by the definition of rape in most states, although these states generally provide for criminal penalties under other laws if there is no penetration. Several states, including California, specify that the essence of the sex crime is an "outrage" to the person and the feelings of the victim.

In Florida, forced intercourse or forced oral or anal sex is called "sexual battery." Colorado's definition of "sexual assault in the first degree" includes forced intercourse, cunnilingus, fellatio, anal/oral acts, and anal intercourse.

Many states have specific statutory provisions concerning the insertion of foreign objects into the genital or anal openings, so the attacker is hardly left with a defense to your charge of sexual abuse if he forced a weapon rather than his penis into you.

And almost all states have criminal penalties for sexual contact, the deliberate touching or rubbing of your body without your consent.

Given the nature of all crimes as "statutory" beasts, questions like "Can a woman rape a man?" or "Can a woman rape a woman?" are answered by the definition section and other sections of the sexual crimes laws of your state. Almost half the states now have provisions that extend rape and other violent sex crimes to situations in which the male is the victim—all without taking away from the protection of the woman under rape laws.

As with all of law, real life answers aren't always identical with the definitions the law sets forth and, in some cases, injustice results. For example, in the past—and in the present in other countries—some statutory definitions of rape or criminal sexual assault demanded ejaculation. If this did not occur, legally there was no rape. This was the case no matter how cruelly the woman was treated by her attacker, made to submit to forced penetration, or was otherwise abused sexually. Gradually, definitions in the rape laws of many states are recognizing the actual abuses suffered by victims.

Are there any special compensation laws to help rape victims?

Yes!

Many states now have legislation that requires care for rape victims. The hope is that more women will report the crime and that proper evidence will be collected to help convict the criminal.

Florida, Illinois, Minnesota, Nevada, and Ohio are among the states that make it illegal for a hospital to turn away a rape victim for financial or other reasons. In addition, the state of Nevada specifically pays for the treatment of emotional problems resulting from rape, treatment not only for the victim but also for her spouse. The only stipulation Nevada makes is that the victim file a rape complaint to be eligible for reimbursement.

Some states, including Minnesota, Illinois, and California, have special victim assistance laws that provide for reimbursement of the rape victim and the hospital for the cost of hospital treatment— examination, evidence preservation, and follow-up VD and pregnancy tests. Other states have more general laws that provide reimbursement of hospital expenses for victims of violent crimes, but rape is among the crimes included. Not every hospital is aware of this legislation. So, if yours is not, check with local women's groups or your state representative. You may be entitled to a refund for hospital services.

Organizations such as the Citizens Committee for Victim Assistance (CCVA), a Chicago-based group, work with the police and hospital administrators to educate them about the availability of emergency room refunds and to instruct them on how and what evidence should be gathered. In conjunction with the Chicago police force, for example, the CCVA designed an evidence preservation kit and then distributed the kits to the emergency rooms of city hospitals.

Community action to prevent rape is meeting with more governmental support, too. If you live in a large housing complex and are always in fear of what could be lurking in those winding corridors, you should call the FBI. Not for an investigation but for information about how you can get funding to provide safer access to your apartment. The FBI will tell you how several government agencies can foot the bill for "sub-dividing" the complex to allow lower-level—and safer—entry into the building.

I was raped while waiting for a train. Since it was dark and there were no transit or security personnel in attendance at the train station, I feel the transit company is responsible for what happened to me. Is it?

Maybe!

The notion that someone else, through negligence, may have "set the stage" for a rape or other violent crime is being recognized as valid in the courts.

You obviously cannot charge the transit company with rape. But you can charge that third party with a personal injury suit, the same legal action you would probably take if you were in any accident resulting from another's negligence. And, on that basis, a woman who was raped in a station of the Southeastern Pennsylvania Transportation Authority successfully sued. A similar action is pending against Greyhound.

As in any other personal injury suit, the person or company you're suing must have had a duty to act and must have breached that legal duty. When you rented your apartment, for example, you may have been impressed by the strong, locking corridor door separating your floor from the lobby. Depending on your state, your landlord may have a duty to keep that lock in good repair. Say the lock breaks. You've notified your landlord of that fact and he doesn't fix it within a reasonable time. If you are then raped by an attacker who otherwise would have been restrained by that locked door, your landlord may be liable. Broken porch lights have launched this kind of litigation too.

But the "breach of duty" has to be the "proximate cause" of your rape, as is the case with any suit for negligence. Say that not being able to get through that broken door made you late for your ride to a party, so you had to walk. While you were walking to the party, you were raped. Even though the broken door was, in one sense, a "real" factor in what happened to you, it wasn't legally a direct cause of the attack.

Who other than your landlord may have this kind of duty? A common carrier—bus, train, or airplane—has historically had an extremely important duty to protect its patrons from injury. That duty requires the carrier company to provide adequate lighting as well as adequate personnel, so that facilities are reasonably free of the threat of rape and other violent crimes.

Index

FBI, 119
federal law, x
Federal Trade Commission, xi
food stamps, 56
fornication, 1
fourteenth amendment, 65

G

gay rights, 45–46
government contracts, 42–43, 44
guardians, 33

H

harassment, sexual, 57–61
hearings, 50–51
home issues, xii, 1–38
homeowner's insurance, 89–90
homestead rights, 6
hot-lines (*see* telephone services)

I

income, 8–10, 15
income tax (*see* taxes)
Individual Retirement Accounts,
    81–82
Internal Revenue Service (*see* taxes)
inheritances (*see* wills)
insurance, 6–7, 80, 87–92
    unemployment, 61–72
issues, xii–xiii

L

land (*see* real estate)
landlords, 120

law
    common, x, 11–12
    contracts, 8
    federal, x
    state, x
    structure of, x–xii
lawsuits, x, 50–53, 106–108,
    119–120
lawyers, ix, 8, 48, 50–53, 99,
    104–105
legal aid, ·104–105
legislation, x
lesbianism, 21, 45–46, 82
licenses
    driver's, 11
    marriage, 10
life insurance, 87–89
loans, 92, 95, 100–101

M

marketplace issues, xii–xiii, 87–102
marriage, 7–10, 93–98
    common-law, 2–3
marriage contracts, 7–9
marriage licenses, 10
medical issues, 27–32
minors, 29–31
morality legislation, 1, 2
mortgages, 4–5

N

National Abortion Rights Action
    League, 31
National Alliance for Displaced
    Homemakers, 57
National Commission on Working
    Women, 54